Scholar -Statesman
SHANKER DAYAL SHARMA

President Dr Shanker Dayal Sharma

Scholar-Statesman
SHANKER DAYAL SHARMA
A Biography

S. C. BHATT

GYAN PUBLISHING HOUSE
NEW DELHI-110002

GYAN PUBLISHING HOUSE
5, Ansari Road, Daryaganj
New Delhi-110002

ISBN—81-212-0430-5

PRINTED IN INDIA

Published by Mrs. Gayatri Garg for Gyan Publishing House, New Delhi 110002
Composed by Ideal Computers Pvt. Ltd., Delhi 110007
Printed at Goyal Offset Works

CONTENTS

PREFACE

When I undertook work on this biography of Dr. Shanker Dayal Sharma I was vaguely aware of the paucity of available biographical material. I knew that I could not expect much help from published sources in completing the task in an extremely short time. But as I went about the job the paucity turned out to be even more acute than I had imagined. Although Dr Sharma has long been on the political scene of the country and is, in many ways, one of the few surviving links with the pre-independence days, surprisingly not much has been written about him. What had been written was often found to be inaccurate when the facts were checked and in some respects the material was delightfully vague.

Fortunately, a number of persons who have watched him at different stages in his career and had known him at close quarters, were willing to talk. Among them I should mention Mr S. Jaipal Reddy, former leader of Opposition in the Rajya Sabha and now leader of the Janata Dal in the House, and senior journalist, Mr K.P. Srivastava. Mr Reddy's observations were pertinent in assessing the role of Dr Sharma as Chairman of the Rajya Sabha, a major chapter in his life. Mr Srivastava had known Dr Sharma while he was posted as PTI correspondent in Bhopal when Dr Sharma's star was just rising. Srivastava later kept contacts with him in Delhi.

Mrs Indira Swaroop of the Madhya Pradesh Information Centre in Delhi not only suggested names of people who could throw light on Dr Sharma's life but made excellent source material available from Bhopal. The Research and Reference Division Library, in Shastri Bhavan in Delhi, placed their books and reference materials at my disposal. The staff helped in tracing references in published books and old magazines and saved me much time and effort. The Press Information Bureau made available their old records and cuttings files. The PIB, Photo Division and the Madhya Pradesh information people, through Mrs Swaroop's intervention, gave me access to their photographic collections. The reference section of AIR's News Services Division traced some important references for me.

To all of them my grateful thanks are due. Above all, I am grateful to my friend, G.N.S. Raghavan, who has made this book possible. He also gave me some useful material. Dr Vijay Aggarwal of the Vice President's office extended assistance for which I am grateful.

Needless to say, the conclusions and assessment are my own and I alone am responsible for any mistakes or inaccuracies. In portraying Dr Sharma's life and his activities in his various capacities, it has been my endeavour to draw a portrait of the man and his rise from humble beginnings to the highest office in the land. The weak spots have not been slurred over and, without indulging in adulation, some of the misconceptions about his role at crucial moments have been dispelled.

S.C. BHATT

1

THE MAN FROM MADHYA PRADESH

Madhya Pradesh, as we know it now, came into being on November 1, 1956 when the States were reorganised. It is located between lattitude 18°N and 26.75°N and between Longitude 74.15°E and 84.25°E. In the north it is bounded by Uttar Pradesh, in the east by Bihar and Orissa, in the south-east by Andhra Pradesh, in the south by Maharashtra and in the west by Gujarat and Rajasthan.

In terms of area, it is the largest State in the country, extending over 4,42,841 sq.kms. In terms of population it is the fifth largest State in the country.[1]

In the words of an outstanding political leader of Madhya Pradesh and its first Chief Minister, Ravi Shankar Shukla:

> "Stretching from the Yamuna to the Godavari new Madhya Pradesh will be the largest State in India, not only in geographical terms but a fusion of many ancient cultures, history and tradition of our country. The granaries of Malwa and the mineral wealth of Madhya Bharat and Vindya Pradesh will make the State prosperous ...I am sure that, situated as it is in the heart of the country, it will become a pillar of strength for the nation".[2]

It is from this Madhya Pradesh State that a person of humble origin at present to become the First Citizen of India. Shanker Dayal Sharma is not only the first President of India from Madhya Pradesh, 20 years ago he had another first to his credit, among the many firsts in his career. In 1972 he became the first President of the Indian National Congress from Madhya Pradesh. A Congress session was held in Tripuri on the bank of the Narmada near Jabalpur in Madhya Pradesh before independence when Subhash Chandra Bose became president of the Congress second time. But Madhya Pradesh had never before given to the nation an outstanding figure of the like of Dr. Sharma.

The State and the region no doubt abound in legend and history and it has been the meeting ground of powerful historical currents. The Dandakaranya forest of the Ramayana is located in the Bastar District of Madhya Pradesh where Rama lived for a considerable time during his years of banishment from Ayodhya. The State has the largest number of rock shelters in the entire country and as many as 25 districts out of the total 45 districts in the State have such shelters. There are paintings of various types on their walls and ceilings. They also speak of the close connection of ancient Madhya Pradesh with Buddhism of which the 'Stupa' at Sanchi near Bhopal and the other near Satna are outstanding examples. No less a person than Emperor Ashoka built these 'Stupas' apart from inscribing inspiring messages in these places and building some rock shelters.

Both in legend and history, the Avanti region centring on Ujjain (Ujjayini of Sanskrit literature) has held an important position in India. It is mentioned in the Puranas as one of the seven great and holy cities of the time.[3] Avanti was one of the 16 great kingdoms in North India at the time of the Buddha. The entire Madhya Pradesh region formed part of the Maurya Empire and Ashoka served as Governor of Avanti before he ascended the imperial throne in Pataliputra (Patna). He is also believed to have married the daughter of a Shreshthi (an affluent businessman), of Vidisha near Bhopal which was another centre of Buddhism at the time of Ashoka monastery built at Vidisha.

Speaking of Madhya Pradesh one cannot help mentioning Kalidasa's close connection with the region. No historical data is available on Kalidasa's life but it is evident that he had minutely studied India's geographical features as evidenced by his writings. In the very first verse of Kumarasambhava he describes the Himalaya mountain as the measuring rod of the earth which has arisen from the oceans on the west and east of India.[4]

But in all his poetic and dramatic works Avanti stands out among the regions of the country with which the great poet was familiar. In Meghaduta, the banished Yaksha is spending his time at Ramagiri, somewhere in Madhya Pradesh. Scholars have identified this place that as Ramgarh in Ambikapur district of the State. Kalidasa shows intimate knowledge of the Vindhya region and the Narmada playing in the foothills of the Vindhya mountains is lovingly described.[5]

In more recent times Gwalior in Madhya Pradesh was the capital of the Sindhia clan of the Marathas who swept over much of the country from their headquarters in Pune. The Sindhia general like Mahadji played an important role in Delhi and north India during the later Mughal period.

Madhya Pradesh, however was not destined to play a major part in history and despite its crucial position at the heart of India it belonged more to the backwaters of the country. The people, however, are with the spirit of Indian culture and its continuity through the ages. They are tolerant, gentle and hard working, although more steeped in tradition.

Madhya Pradesh also has the unique distinction of having the famous Khajuraho temples, which symbolise the fusion of 'Kama' (sex) with life and religion through their sculptures and carvings.

Shanker Dayal overcame the forces of tradition, which hold you in bondage, but imbibed in his mental make up the spirit underlying the traditional values of Indian life. He emerged from this society and went for higher studies to Allahabad and Lucknow where great events of political significance were taking place. While scoring distinctions in his studies he also absorbed the political influences which were later to shape his career and helped him to arrive on the national scene as nobody else from Madhya Pradesh before him had done.

NOTES

1. *Encyclopaedia of India,* Volume III, Madhya Pradesh, Rima Publishing House, New Delhi, 1992.
2. *Ibid*

3.

अयोध्या मथुरा माया काशी कांची अवन्तिक ।
पुरी घरामती चैव सप्तैते मोक्षदायिकाः ।।

"(Ayodhya, Mathura, Maya, Kashi (Varanasi), Kanchi, Avantika and the city of Dwaraka are the seven cities which lead to liberation (Moksha)".

4.

अस्त्युन्तरस्था दिशि देवतात्मा हिमालयो जार नत्राधिराजः ।
पूर्वा परौ तोथनिधीऽ वत्राह्य स्थितः पृथिव्या इव मानदण्डः ।।

"There, in the northern direction, is the king of mountains, Himalaya, the spirit of divinity, which is like the measuring rod of the earth, having risen from the oceans on the east and west."

Kumarasambhaya 1.1

5. In *Meghaduta*, Kalidasa refers to the Avanti region in which the great city of Ujjayini is located and which he compares almost with heaven because those who have exhausted their merit and are descending from heaven come to live in the city.

Purva-Megha 30

2

EARLY LIFE AND PURSUIT OF SCHOLARSHIP

Madhya Pradesh by its very name means the central region of India. At the centre of Madhya Pradesh is Bhopal, the capital of the State since November, 1956, and at the heart of old Bhopal is the thickly populated Guliya Dai Ka Mohalla. Here in the ancestral home of Pandit Khushilal Sharma, Shanker Dayal was born on August 19, 1918.

Khushilal was a noted vaidya, an ayurvedic physician, who ran his clinic from his residence. A great devotee of Lord Shiva and a deeply religious man, he named his first born child after his favourite deity and called him Shanker Dayal.

According to some accounts written by admirers, astrologers predicted a great future for the child and told

Khushilal that his son would one day occupy a high position in the country. What kind of a future the vaidya could have visualised for his son at a time when the country was in subjugation? The first world war was about to end and the country was soon to be plunged in a major national struggle under Mahatma Gandhi's leadership. But no astrological predictions were necessary for the father to realise that he and his wife Subhadra had begotten a highly intelligent and studious child.

From his days in the Ramakrishna Pathshala, where he had his schooling in Bhopal, Shanker Dayal displayed scholarship of a high order. Bhai Ratan Kumar, who was Shanker Dayal's fellow student in the primary school and also later-on in the college, has in an article noted:

> "From his childhood I have watched him strive for excellence. He could not tolerate anything but the highest position in any activity he undertook, whether it was a matter of studies or swimming or chess or any other sport in which he was interested. Not only he acquired the highest degrees during his student days at Agra, Allahabad and Lucknow, he also won the topmost position in swimming and other sports elocution and so on. Because of his alround ability, Shanker Dayal won the Chakravorti Gold Medal in Lucknow University. His urge always to be in the highest position is reflected in an incident which I recall when both of us went to a book stall at the Bhopal Railway station to see our results in the intermediate examination in the day's newspaper. He flunged the newspaper aside. He had scored the 2nd division instead of the first in that examination."[1]

From Bhopal, Shanker Dayal went to Agra and joined the St. John's College for his B.A. degree. He was, however, no bookworm and had a wide range of interests in literature and sports. Ratan Kumar and another student from Bhopal called Alim shared a room with him in the hostel. Ratan Kumar recalls how Shanker Dayal read his poems with avidity and a particular line in one of his composition *'Takat Apni, Taul Sipahi, armanose Baledano se'*.- (Soldier of freedom, measure your strength against your aspirations and your sacrifices) particularly appealed to Shanker Dayal. In 1973 when he was felicitated by people in Bhopal on his election as President of the Indian National Congress, Sharma recalled this line.

Ratan Kumar has also recorded another characteristic of the young Shanker Dayal:

> "A significant trait of Dr. Shanker Dayal Sharma has been his capacity to study in depth and acquire complete mastery over any new subject he took up, or any task which was assigned to him. This gave him unusual success in life. He was never scared of undertaking difficult assignments. Because of his religious faith, he has immense self-confidence and capacity to carry out difficult tasks.' He has wonderful physical and mental capabilities.[2]

Ratan Kumar had not only been a fellow student of Shanker Dayal for many years but he was already involved in political activities in Bhopal. When Shanker Dayal returned from abroad in 1948, he was one of the local political activists who invited Shanker Dayal to take part in the agitation for the merger of Bhopal, then a princely State, with the rest of India and both spent time together in the Bhopal Central Jail, during that struggle details of which have been examined in the Chapter 'At the helm in Bhopal'.[3]

From Agra Dr. Sharma went to Allahabad to study at Allahabad University and later on he enrolled himself at Lucknow University in the capital city of the then United Provinces, now called Uttar Pradesh. From there he took his M.A.degrees in English literature, Hindi and Sanskrit and was first in the University. He went on to obtain LL.M from the same University and again secured the first position.

Because of the limited resources of the family his studies were mostly prosecuted with the help of scholarships but his step- mother, Sampathbai, had to pawn her jewellery to help Shanker Dayal go abroad for further studies. Shanker Dayal went from Lucknow to Cambridge University in the United Kingdom and joined the Fitzwilliam College in that University to acquire his Ph D. degree in Law. He taught Law both at Lucknow and Cambridge. While at Cambridge, he also added to the illustrious lists of degrees earned by him. He was called to the Bar from Lincoln s Inn and also got a diploma in Public Administration. For some time he was a Fellow at the Harvard Law School in the United States.

His mother Subhadra had taught him Hindi and Sanskrit at home while he was at school in Bhopal. His first lessons in the Ramayana, Mahabharata, the Bhagawat Purana as well as the Sanskrit lexicon Amarakosha were learnt at the feet of his mother.

From his father he imbided the spirit of service to humanity and deep desire to be of help to fellow human beings. His father also took him everyday to the famous lake in Bhopal for a swim and for his morning ablutions. While on the way to the lake the father taught his young son how to master the intricacies of the Sanskrit language. His deep interest in swimming acquired from his home town helped him to win a swimming competition in Lucknow University. In Bhopal where Shanker Dayal has over the years become a kind of a legend, people still talk of how father and son took a measure of the small lake and then the big lake.

After the death of his mother Subhadra at a young age his father married Sampatbai, a cousin of his first wife. Shanker Dayal was then in college and could not be present at the wedding. The step-mother and the son took to each other as though he was her own son. Sampatbai recalls the close affinity between them:

> "I didn't have any trouble in adjusting because my husband's first wife was my cousin sister. I used to visit her often in this house (Guliya Dai's Mohalla). I knew him (Shanker Dayal) before my marriage. There are just a few years between us. There was a tradition in our house of not calling the eldest son by his name. He was called '*Bhaiya*!. I also began calling him *Bhaiya* and he calls me '*Chachi*'. All my children, grandchildren, patients, vegetable vendors and who ever visits my house also call me *chachi*."[4]

Sampatbai at the age of 80 has been practising as an Ayurvedic physician. She was taught the Indian system of medicine by her husband and later she acquired a proper degree also. Before her marriage Shanker Dayal and a sister Rukmani were born in the house, of the first wife Subhadra. Sampatbai has four sons. Shambu Dayal, 52, who is the eldest of the four brothers, Shiv Dayal, Ish Dayal and Somesh Dayal 43, the youngest. They all live in Bhopal and are greatly fond of '*Dadabhai*' as Shanker Dayal is called in the family.

Shanker Dayal lost his first wife who resided with their child, a son called Satish, in the ancestral house in

Bhopal, while the young Shanker Dayal was pursuing his studies in various universities. When Shanker Dayal returned from abroad after completing his education and taught at the Law School in Lucknow University, Sampatbai persuaded him to marry again. Shanker Dayal and Vimla were married in 1950.

Vimla Sharma who has been Dr. Shanker Dayal Sharma's constant campanion for the past many years and has been in public view, time and again, during the years when he was the Vice President of India, is a woman in her own rights. She was among the first women to receive a University degree and even do post- Graduation in Jaipur in the forties in Rajputana, as Rajasthan was then known. The area was strongly under the influence of orthodoxy and women education, especially higher education, was not much prevalent. She has distinguished herself in her own way in social work but more than anything else she has been an ideal wife.[5]

Besides, Satish, who was born of his first wife, the Sharmas had three children - daughters Jaishree and Geetanjali and a son Ashutosh. Geetanjali was killed by the Punjab terrorists along with her husband Lalit Makin in Delhi in 1985.

Shanker Dayal was brought up in a typically Hindu middle-class family in what was then a provincial town. The family had homogeneity and not only has Sampatbai been the presiding deity of the joint family but there has been no distinction of real or step brothers. Neither has the fact that the eldest brother captured one milestone after another in the pursuit of his political career affected the relationship between Shanker Dayal and the rest of the family.

Shanker Dayal's sister Rukmani, now 70, suffered a paralytic stroke following a brain haemorrhage a few years ago and is now confined to bed. Shambhu Dayal, the eldest of the four sons of Sampatbai, and his other brothers all live in Bhopal. Shanker Dayal's daughter Jayashree is married to Vinod Sharma, now a Congress (I) member of the Rajya Sabha from Punjab. Ashotosh holds a senior executive position in a private business house.

For 23 years, Dr. Sharma has been having with him an aide, who has been almost a part of the family. J.N. Kashyap who began life as a local politician in Delhi joined Shanker Dayal when he was President of the Indian National Congress in 1973 and the association there-after became so close that Kashyap, although he belongs to the Scheduled Caste community, has access to every part of the household of Shanker Dayal Sharma, whether it is the prayer room or the kitchen.

As President of the Congress, Shanker Dayal had Aziza Imam - a Muslim, Mrs. M. Chandrasekharan, - a Scheduled Caste and Chandrajit Yadav from socially and educationally backward classes as his general secretaries. Both Yadav and Chandrasekharan are now Members of the Lok Sabha, the former belonging to the Janata Dal and the later Congress(I).

While in Lucknow University, Dr. Shanker Dayal Sharma had come into close contact with Acharya Narendra Deva, who was then Vice-Chancellor of the University. Narendra Deva was a top leader of the Congress and also founded the Congress Socialist Party along with Jayaprakash Narayan.

Dr. Sharma had to shuttle between Lucknow and Bhopal where he was already drawn into the vortex of politics. Narendra Deva not only encouraged him in his political activities but also helped him by granting him leave from his position as Lecturer/Reader in the Law

School of the University from time to time. Finally the time came for Sharma to say good-bye to his alma mater where he had become a teacher also. On his election as President of the Bhopal Congress and subsequently as Chief Minister of the State he had to bid good-bye to academic life.

NOTES

1. Article "Uprashtrapati, Dr. Shanker Dayal Sharma" in *Madhya Pradesh Sandesh*, Nov. 1987.
2. *Ibid*
3. *Ibid.*
4. Interview in *Sunday Mail*, Delhi, July 12, 1992 by Swapna Majumdar.
5. *Hindu*, Delhi edition, July 17, 1992.

3

AT THE HELM IN BHOPAL

On October 16, 1948, Shanker Dayal returned to Bhopal from abroad after acquiring a string of high academic qualifications. But before he could leave for Lucknow University to resume his duties as a lecturer in the Law Department of his own alma mater, he was beckond by a major political development in his own town.

Bhopal was one of the princely States of India, 550 odd, which had become nominally independent on India's independence. The integration of these States with India was one of the outstanding developments in the first few years of freedom for which the credit mainly goes to Sardar Patel, a great leader of the freedom movement who became Deputy Prime Minister on independence. In Bhopal the people wanted that the State which was ruled by a Nawab should merge with the rest of India and become a part of the national mainstream. The Nawab who had other ideas and had been the president of the Chamber of Princes, just before independence, wanted Bhopal to continue to be a separate State. He had brought into being a showpiece of an advisory Council of nominated political leaders, but that did not satisfy the people.

The youth in particular were keen to be led by Shanker Dayal in a non-violent struggle against the Nawab to secure his agreement for the merger of the State with the rest of India. The struggle was launched and Dr. Sharma emerged as an inspiring leader of a popular movement. His baptisim in the political field in a popular cause really laid the foundation of his career as a public man.

Dr. Shanker Dayal suffered imprisonment and many men and women went to jail with him, several suffered *lathi* blows and a few laid down their lives. On June 1, 1949, Bhopal merged with India. Summing up the achievements of the struggle, Shanker Dayal wrote in a journal:

> "The people of Bhopal gave a good account of themselves in the merger campaign. This was a struggle unique in itself. After Bapu's death the Bhopal people for the first time applied his technique of truth and non-violence and achieved success. The authorities committed all kinds of excesses in order to provoke the people and turned them towards violence. The police picked up children, mothers and sisters were also not spared. Prostitutes were used against us and fire engines were deployed. The people, however, bravely bore *lathi* blows and faced the bullets of the Nawab's police. Precious lives were sacrificed but the path of non-violence was not given up. I am proud of being a son of this soil."[1]

At the successful conclusion of the merger struggle, Dr. Sharma was back in Lucknow in the academic world, which he loved much. Although he had acquired the degree of Bar-at-Law, he had not thought of starting legal practice and preferred the life of a teacher to practice at the Bar. He was, however, not destined to stay in Lucknow for long as the call of duty came from Bhopal once again.

His success in the merger movement had made Shanker Dayal popular with the people of Bhopal but some sections of the political activists of the small State were not too keen that he should join active politics. Dissidence in the Congress ranks was prevalent even then and Shanker Dayal had his first taste of the infighting in the party as he contested the election to the Presidentship of the Bhopal Congress.

In spite of the activities of those who did not relish his advent into Bhopal politics, Shanker Dayal was unanimously elected President of the Bhopal Congress on January 11, 1951.

General Elections were due early in 1952 for the first Lok Sabha to be elected under the Constitution and the various State Assemblies. Bhopal as a part 'C' State was also to have its own Assembly of 30 members and the Congress High Command with Jawaharlal Nehru as President decided that Shanker Dayal should run for the State Assembly. He chose the Bairasiya constituency from which he was returned after a stiff contest.[2] His opponent was M.G. Poddar, manager of the only textile mill in Bhopal, who had the support of the powerful business lobby. Dr. Shanker Dayal's opponents in the party were also believed to be working for his defeat.

Not only did Shanker Dayal win his own seat, the Congress won a big majority in the small Bhopal Assembly and again in the selection of Assembly party leader the

Congress central leadership clearly indicated its preference for Dr. Shanker Dayal. In fact that was what the people and ordinary party workers also wanted, although a group had already come into being under the leadership of Kampta Prasad[3], who was an aspirant for the position of the first Chief Minister of Bhopal. On political considerations and the advise of local leaders, Dr. Sharma, however, tried to pacify Prasad by including him in his small cabinet of four persons. The other three, besides himself as Chief Minister, were Maulana Tarzi Mashriq, Kamta Prasad and Umrao Singh. Even in those days, Dr. Sharma fully understood the importance of having the representatives of the minorities and Scheduled Castes in the Government, Umrao Singh being from the Scheduled Castes community.

Dr. Sharma was a fast learner and made up for his administrative inexperience by willingness to be guided by experienced administrators from the I.C.S. (Indian Civil Service) and by his intense desire to improve the living conditions of his people. When he took over as Chief Minister in March 19, 1952, a senior civilian S. Viswanathan was Bhopal's chief commissioner[4]. He was soon transferred and was replaced by another I.C.S. officer, Bhagwan Sahay, who was not only well versed in administration but also an extrovert, a connoisser of literature and the finer things of life. A good rapport developed between Sharma and Bhagwan Sahay and not only did Sharma acquired the tricks of the trade from him but also Sahay's presence in Bhopal proved beneficial to him because the Centre got the right feedback during Dr. Sharma's tenure. Sahay had a good standing with the Central Government and with Nehru.

Early in life, Dr. Sharma proved that he was imbued with a keen desire to serve the people, had an open mind in acquiring expertise from those who had it and showed himself capable of establishing a good rapport with senior administrators. He also understood fast the crooked ways of politics, which helped him to defeat the designs of his political opponents within his own party.

He kept an open mind and listened to the advise of political workers and those who had spent years in public life The appreciation which he had received from leaders in Delhi was proving useful to him not only politically but also in acquiring resources for the development of Bhopal. Whereas Vindhya Pradesh, with a population of 40 lakhs was getting Central assistance worth Rs. 3 crores per year, Bhopal with just 8 lakh people was receiving from the Centre assistance worth Rs. 5 to Rs. 10 crores every year[5].

He invited industrialists from Bombay and elsewhere to set up industries in Bhopal. The presence of Sindhi refugees at Bairagarh, near Bhopal, led to increased commercial activities in the State. Shanker Dayal's endeavours and his rapport with the Centre helped in setting up of a regional engineering college, a medical college, a polytechnic and an agriculture college in and around Bhopal. In 1957 the foundation of the Bhopal-based Bharat Heavy Electricals (BHEL) was laid by the then Commerce and Industry Minister in the Nehru Government, Morarji Desai. But Shanker Dayal had worked continuously to ensure that this major project came to Bhopal.

Dissident activities were continuing all the time in the small Assembly party and Kampta Prasad led a deputation to Nehru but without any success. In fact, Dr. Sharma had by now established such close relations with the Central leaders that Nehru visited Bhopal more than once during Shanker Dayal's tenure as Chief Minister. The President, Dr. Rajendra Prasad, also made an official visit to the small State and a Union Minister, Lal Bahadur Shastri, whose importance was known even then, was also among the visitors from Delhi. Shanker Dayal in the meanwhile worked to the target of a school in every village, a middle school in every Panchayat and a higher Secondary school in every small town. Medical facilities were also being expanded[6].

The States Reorganisation Commission (SRC) under Justice Fazle Ali and with K.M. Panikkar and Hirday Nath Kunzru as members had been appointed by the Centre to redraw the political map of India. What is Madhya Pradesh today was then split into four different parts - Madhya Pradesh which was the new name of the old province of C.P. (Central Provinces) and Berar, Madhya Bharat, consisting mainly of the former Gwalior State, Vindya Pradesh, with Rewa as its capital and comparatively smaller Bhopal State. It was on the cards that a bigger Madhya Pradesh consisting of these fair units would be born out of the labours of the SRC.

What was of special interest to the people of the future Madhya Pradesh was where would be the capital of the State. When the SRC's recommendations came, it was found that the Commission had chosen Jabalpur as the capital of a new Madhya Pradesh State. There was no doubt that Jabalpur was a well developed major urban area in the whole State but there were other rivals like Gwalior and, above all, Bhopal.

It was left to Shanker Dayal to lobby the Central leadership in Delhi to ensure that Bhopal became the capital of the new State, rather than Jabalpur. It was an uphill task to convince the then Home Minister, Govind Ballabh Pant, to effect a change in the SRC's recommendations but Shanker Dayal worked ceaselessly to make Bhopal a focal point of a larger State. In this a number of favourable factors were also going to prove of help to him. The fact that

Bhopal was more centrally located than any other city in the larger Madhya Pradesh worked to its advantage. Its population, with a large number of Muslims in the former princely State, helped to convince Nehru that it would be in the interest of Madhya Pradesh to locate the capital there.

Finally, Bhopal was chosen and the infrastructure for a State secretariat had to be considerably developed. The High Court was, however, located in Jabalpur. Bhopal with its two lakes, the big lake and the small one, in both of which Shanker Dayal had his first lessons in swimming from his father, were a special attraction to anyone looking for a good city as the central point of Madhya Pradesh, the largest Indian State in terms of geographical area.

Pandit Ravi Shankar Shukla, who had been a Minister and then Prime Minister (as Chief Ministers were known in the days of provincial autonomy in British India) before independence and was Chief Minister of the erstwhile Madhya Pradesh State was the unanimous choice for the office of Chief Minister of the enlarged Madhya Pradesh. Dr. Shanker Dayal Sharma was included in the cabinet which came into being in November 1956 and was given charge of the education portfolio. He continued to be a Minister of Cabinet rank in the new State after the 1957 and 1962 Assembly elections.

In addition to Education he also held the charge of Law, Public Works, Industries and Commerce from time to time. His excellent academic record and administrative experience that he had gained in running a small but a separate State for more than four years stood him in good stead in his career as a senior Minister in Madhya Pradesh.

His innate ability to make friends, establish a good working relationship with civil servants and his clean image as a public man marked him out as an outstanding figure in Madhya Pradesh. His emphasis on development was so great that some observers felt he was sacrifising quality at the altar of quantity. In the new Madhya Pradesh, Dr. Sharma occupied three major positions, Education Minister, Industry Minister and Minister of Public Works. Madhya Pradesh today has an industrial estate in every district and a network of higher secondary schools at the Tehsil level has been established. Dr. Sharma's policy is : 'expand'. Dr. Sharma lays more emphasis on quantity than on quality.[6] Yet another writer pointed out that Dr. Sharma was the first Education Minister in any State in India to introduce a number of development schemes:

> "The development of education in Madhya Pradesh received a fillup (at Dr. Sharma's hands). Dr. Sharma introduced proper pay scales for teachers for the first time in the country. Other States followed suit. Once I pointed out to him that he was moving at a fast pace in expanding education, the result was that there was as much confusion as expansion. His reply was very straightforward, 'Mayaramji, there must be development. This confusion is temporary"[7].

As Chief Minister of Bhopal as well as Minister of Education in the enlarged Madhya Pradesh State, Dr. Sharma laid special emphasis on the development of Hindi language and personally attended literary conferences and poetic symposia or 'Kavi Sammelan'. It was a tribute to his efforts to popularise literature, while thousands of people attended the symposia and enjoyed an interface with men and women of literature.

in the growth of Urdu. Once a local newspaper, *Navbharat*, carried a story on the 'death' of a noted Urdu poet Sheri Bhopali. The poet had composed a popular ghazal which had been sung by many well known singers but he seems to have got little of it. Actually Sheri was not dead but *Navbharat* wanted to highlight the fact that the poet was in a bad way and would, in fact, die if help was not rushed to him.

Dr. Sharma was so moved by the story of the penurious condition of the Urdu poet that he immediately put him in the State Government's employment so that he could make two ends meet.

In 1967, the Congress lost power in several States and S.V.D. (Sanyukta Vidhayak Dal) governments of opposition parties coming together to form an alternatve ministry came into being in Madhya Pradesh as well as in some other States. Dr. Sharma was not, however, at a loose end. He had by now established himself as a senior leader in the State. Political denigration of successful men, especially those who do not distribute patronage on a lavish scale, goes on all the time and Dr. Sharma was no exception to this process. However, his position of eminence in the party ensured that the crown of Madhya Pradesh Congress Committee was placed on his head in 1967. To be elected President of the Congress in a major State when he was not yet fifty and considering that he belonged to no group, was a recognition of his high status in the party.

NOTES

1. Quoted in an article "I am proud to be a son of this soil" by Syed Ali Hassan Mujeeb in *Madhya Pradesh Sandesh*, Bhopal, November, 1987.
2. See Chapter on Dr. S.D. Sharma in "Mukhya Mantri Madhya Pradesh ke" by Mayaram Surjan, *Radhakrishna Prakashan*, Delhi, 1991.

3. *Ibid*
4. *Ibid*
5. Thakur Vijay Singh "Vijay", in *Madhya Pradesh Sandesh,* November, 1987.
6. Devendra Khare in *Madhya Pradesh Sandesh,* November, 1987.
7. Mayaram Surjan, *Op. Cit.* Chapter on Dr. Shanker Dayal Sharma.

4

THE CONGRESS SPLIT

From the time Jawaharlal Nehru called upon Shanker Dayal in 1952 to take over the leadership of the Congress party in Bhopal, Shanker Dayal had begun what turned out to be a long association with the Congress. During his years in office first as Chief Minister of Bhopal State, from March 1952 to October 1956, and then as a Cabinet Minister in the enlarged Madhya Pradesh State, with which Bhopal had merged, from October 1956 to March 1967, he continued his association with the party.

Then in December 1967, Shanker Dayal was elected President of the Madhya Pradesh Congress Committee. This was a major responsibility as Madhya Pradesh was a big State whose different segments had to be gradually integrated into a whole. But he had occupied this position for hardly a year when he was called to higher responsibilities in the party. After the Hyderabad session of the Congress, the party President, Mr. S. Nijalingappa, nominated Dr. Sharma as a member of the Congress Working Committee (CWC) and later appointed him as one of the General Secretaries of the AICC.

At this stage it would be appropriate to take stock of the split in the Congress party.[1,2,3]

S. Nijalingappa, then Chief Minister of Mysore (now part of Karnataka) was elected President of the Indian National Congress on December 7, 1967 uncontested after four other candidates in the field withdrew from the contest. They were Gulzari Lal Nanda, S.K. Patil, Mohan Dharia and K. Hanumanthaiah. Although the election was "unanimous", there was tension within the party and two distinct groups were emerging. One consisted of the newly elected President and other members of the old guard like S.K. Patil, Morarji Desai, K. Kamaraj and Atulya Ghosh. The other was led by Mrs. Indira Gandhi who had once more become Prime Minister in March 1967. It comprised prominent persons like Fakhurddin Ali Ahmed, C. Subramaniam and some of the "Young Turks".

A number of policy issues were being raised but the crux of the conflict was whether the Prime Minister would be given a free hand in running the Government and in formulating its policies or be subject to the guidance of the organisational leaders. However, the current problems were sorted out and the Hyderabad session of the Congress put up a show of unity. Apart from seven persons elected to the Congress Working Committee the President nominated 13 other members to the committee. Among, them were Prime Minister Indira Gandhi, Deputy Prime Minister Morarji Desai, Jagjivan Ram, Y. B. Chavan, K. Kamaraj, Fakhurddin Ali Ahmed and Shanker Dayal Sharma.

Interestingly, there was friction between the party President and the Prime Minister over the nominations but Dr. Sharma came into the highest forum of the party without a whiff of controvercy. He was already President of the PCC of a major State like Madhya Pradesh and had also had a successful tenure as a Minister. Shanker Dayal now emerged as a political figure of importance. Not only did Nijalingappa nominate him to the CWC but he also appointed Sharma as one of the General Secretaries of the party.

Indira Gandhi had wanted Dinesh Singh and Uma Shankar Dikshit, along with some others, to be nominated to the Working Committee. She had not been able to get any one of her choice elected among the seven elected members of the committee and except C. Subramaniam there was none among them whom she could count as her supporter. She was, therefore, keen to get some of her known and trusted supporters into the CWC through nomination. Nijalingappa, however, was in no mood to oblige her as far as Dinesh Singh was concerned. He considered Dinesh Singh inexperienced and young but he agreed to nominate Dikshit to meet Mrs. Gandhi's wishes halfway.

Matters came to a head in the middle of 1969 when the incumbent President of the Indian Republic, Dr. Zakir Hussain died and the party had to select its nominee for the office of the Head of State. Mrs. Gandhi was keen on the nomination of Jagjivan Ram while Nijalingappa and the old guard, nicknamed "Syndicate", were favouring Neelam Sanjiva Reddy. Indira had to bow to the wishes of the old guard and herself proposed Sanjiva Reddy as the party candidate when the time for filing nominations came.

She was, however, not reconciled to the situation and fought back. First, she relieved Morarji Desai, Deputy Prime Minister, of the Finance portfolio on July 14 whereupon Desai resigned from the Cabinet in protest. She herself took over the Finance portfolio to give "impetus to her new economic policies". As part of that, she nationalised 14 leading banks through an ordinance on July 19, 1967. After he had signed the ordinance, Mr. V.V. Giri, the acting President of India, resigned and announced his candidature for the office of President as an independent.

The rift between Indira Gandhi and the party's old guard - the syndicate - was widening. In the process Sanjiva Reddy faced a strong rival in Giri whom Mrs. Indira Gandhi and her supporters now favoured in preference to the party candidate. There was also a third contestant, Chintaman D. Deshmukh, who was supported by the Swantantra Party and the Jana Sangh.

It was inevitable that such cataclysmic developments should stir the party to its depth. Not only the partymen had voted for two different candidates in the presidential election, but the Prime Minister and her supporters had also openly campaigned for Giri and against the party candidate Sanjiva Reddy.

Dr. Sharma who was the party General Secretary had to choose between the old guard and Mrs. Indira Gandhi who had a special appeal to the younger elements in the party. Ideologically, he found himself close to the thinking of Mrs. Gandhi and saw in her actions the possibility of the fulfilment of his cherished dream, the removal of India's poverty.

It was not surprising, therefore, that Shanker Dayal was one of the three members of the Working Committee who were removed from their position by party President

Nijalingappa. The other two were Fakhurddin Ali Ahmed and C. Subramaniam.

Moves and countermoves were in progress. Nijalingappa and the old guard proposed stern action against Mrs. Gandhi. Her supporters asked for a requisitioned meeting of the AICC. (Hence the name Congress R, for requisition, after the split, while the Congress represented by Nijalingappa's supporters was called Congress O, organisation). Nijalingappa did not concede this demand and the battlelines were being drawn. Mrs. Gandhi had a majority of the party MPs behind her while some of the party fora were lined behind the old guard.

A humorous event took place early in November that year when both sides called a meeting of what they considered was the Congress Working Committee. Of the 21 members exactly ten each attended one or the other rival meeting and one member, K.C. Abraham, from Kerala, attended the Prime Minister's meeting in the morning and then went over to the one held in the party office at 7, Jantar Mantar road, under the chairmanship of the party President Nijalingappa.

For Shanker Dayal the path was clearly taking him in the direction of Indira Gandhi. He was now nominated, along with Fakhruddin and Subramaniam, by Mrs. Gandhi's group to a three man preparatory committee for the requisitioned AICC meeting and for other activities of the new party, or the Congress (R), as it came to be known.

Shanker Dayal was the obvious choice for the office of party general secretary in the new set-up for which his experience as general secretary of the undivided Congress was to stand him in good stead. His equation with Nijalingappa, incidentally, was quite good, contrary to the general belief that they were not getting on too well. As a matter of fact, when Nijalingappa went on an extended foreign tour in 1968 he had taken Sharma with him. It was during their visit to Singapore when both were guests of the Indian High Commissioner, Surendra Sinh Alirajpur, that I met Dr. Sharma for the first time. I interviewed both him and Nijalingappa for ALL INDIA RADIO. I was then AIR's South East Asia correspondent posted in Singapore. Having got to interview both on more or less the same theme, their impressions of their world tour, I requested Nijalingappa to be interviewed in English and Sharma in Hindi Both agreed.

The thinking which took Shanker Dayal to the other side of the fence in the power struggle between the Government and the party is reflected in his writings and speeches of those days. In an article in the *Socialist India*, a Congress party organ, in February 1971, he made a strong plea for the people's support to the Indira party in the forthcoming Lok Sabha poll which resulted in a landslide victory for the party. He wrote[4] :

"The Congress is more than a party. It is a rally of the Indian people — a gathering together of all those elements in national life which are liberal, enlightened, progressive and forward looking, drawn without distinction from peasants and workers, from rural and urban areas and from all walks of life, whose devotion to the country is paramount. The Congress alone has the cohesion, strength, vitality, vision and determination to strive for a nation that is unified, in the ways of social justice, peace and democracy a Government that is stable, strong and efficient and a society of equal opportunity where the strong will not oppress the weak, nor the rich exploit the poor".

After the elections were won he again said[5] : "There is a great responsibility cast not only on the Congress administration, but also on the Congress Organisation to see that the common man does not suffer at the hands of the vested interests and richer sections of society, who can endeavour to take revenge on the poor sections for their assertion against these vested interests."

Sharma continued to speak in the same vein later when in 1972 he was elected President of the party. He said that the monopolies held the dominating heights in spite of recognition of the increasing importance of the public sector.[6] In his presidential address to the AICC in New Delhi on June 1, 1977, Sharma observed that it was regrettable that "Seventyfive monopoly houses control 55 per cent of the assets of the non-banking private corporate sector. Innumerable commissions and inquiries have proved that the monopoly houses are not production oriented but operate on the principle of maximum profits with minimum production, along with black money operation, preemption of licences and collaboration agreements with foreign firms."

He welcomed the nationalisation of fourteen leading banks as a radical measure for making loans available for the farming sector and the employment oriented small-scale industrial undertakings. But he pointed out that the loans were being advanced to the monopoly houses without converting the advances into equity capital. He said that the State did not acquire ownership and management control commensurate with its shareholdings in the monopoly companies.

Thus Shanker Dayal's thinking was in line with, in fact, somewhat ahead of the thinking of the Congress under Mrs. Gandhi's leadership and the question why he chose to go along with Mrs. Gandhi is automatically answered. He also uttered a warning that nationalisation should not be identified with socialism, although there could be no socialism without it.

Again in October 1972, when the AICC met at Gandhinagar in Gujarat, under Dr. Sharma's presidentship, major recommendations on economic policy were made.[7] These included the need for establishment of a Public Distribution System (PDS) to make essential items of mass consumption, like wheat, sugar, edible oils and standard cloth, available to the people at fixed prices, and a major assault on unemployment and poverty. They have become lasting features of national planning over several five year plans.

Speaking at the AICC(I) session in New Delhi on July 1974, Shanker Dayal reminded the partymen that "We have won freedom for our nation and have given it a democratic system. But our pledges to our people are yet to be fulfilled, namely, to win for them their economic freedom."

The point to be stressed here is that there was much thinking on economic development on Sharma's part which brought him closer to Mrs. Gandhi. Many of these assumptions have now been given the go-by under the "new economic policy" but the PDS and the anti-poverty programmes have survived. That alone should prove that Shanker Dayal's thoughts have stood the test of time.

Contrary to the belief entertained by some people that Dr. Sharma jumped on to the populist bandwagon of Indira Gandhi, his was a deliberate choice based on genuine economic policy considerations. That he should have been an automatic choice for membership of the CWC by Nigalingappa while the claims of Uma Shankar Dikshit and Dinesh Singh had to be pressed by Indira would also indicate that he was nobody's protege.

NOTES

For details of the Congress party split the following sources have been consulted :

1. *The Congress Splits* by R.P.Rao, Laivani Publishing House, Bombay 1971
2. *The Congress Splits* by Basant Chatterjee, S. Chand & Co., Delhi, 1970.
3. *Congress Party and Government* by B.B. Misra, Concept Publishing Company, New Delhi, 1988.
4. Quoted in *Congress Party and Social Change* by N.L. Madan, B.R. Publishing Corporation, Delhi, 1984.
5. *Ibid.*
6. *Congress Party and Government* by B.B. Misra, pp 246 following.
7. *Ibid.*

5

CENTRAL MINISTER OF COMMUNICATIONS

As Shanker Dayal completed a two-year term as Congress President in 1974, Prime Minister Indira Gandhi inducted him into her cabinet at the Centre. She gave him the portfolio of Communications as a Cabinet Minister which means responsibility for running post offices, the telegraph and telephone services, the Overseas Communication Service and some public sector undertakings like the Indian Telephone Industries in Bangalore.

In media parlance, Communications is not a "major" portfolio. However, the cabinet was half way in its career by the time Dr. Sharma joined it and there was no vacancy in the major ministries like Finance, Defence, Agriculture and Home. Some senior party leaders with vast administrative experience, including a tenure at the Centre, like Jagjivan Ram and Y.B. Chavan, were already in charge of one or the other major portfolio.

Mrs Gandhi had also not seen Shanker Dayal in action at first hand, as Nehru and Lal Bahadur Shastri had done, when Dr Sharma was playing a prominent role in the shaping of Bhopal and later Madhya Pradesh State. Although he had been a staunch associate in the struggle she had waged against the party old guard in 1969 and later when she ventured out on her own with her slogan of "*garibi hatao*", she had by 1974 another team of advisors in her inner circle, popularly known as the "kitchen cabinet".

Also it must be noted that while Communications is not a "major" portfolio in terms of policy making in the Government, like Home, Finance or Defence, it is of great significance to the economic and social development of the country. Next only to the Railways, the Posts and Telegraph department and the various telecommunications services, under the Ministry of Communications, are the largest employer of manpower. By the time Dr. Sharms left the Ministry in March 1977 the number of such employees, including extra-departmental employees in the post offices and industrial workers in the workshops, was as high as 6.77 lakhs. There was in fact, an increase of nearly half a lakh while he was minister for three years.

Like the Railways and unlike most other ministries including some of the "major" ones, the Communications Ministry is directly run by the Centre. The ministry has no excuses to make, like Home or Agriculture, which often make the pietous plea in Parliament, "we have asked the State concerned for details".

The departments under Communications have seen tremendous expansion. While the people at large remain far from satisfied with the performance of the postal and telecommunications departments, the fact remains that the services have been spread far and wide. There has been a more than threefold increase in the number of post offices and the telephones have multiplied several times more. From 1951 when planning took roots in our country to 1974 when Dr. Sharma became Minister of Communications the number of post offices had risen three times to 1,16,804 (of which rural India accounted for 1,05,491) and by the time he gave up charge the number had again gone up by more than 4,000.[1]

During his tenure a plan to set up post offices in the remote, backward and hilly areas came to be implemented. Even if a post office met only a meagre 15 per cent of the cost of running it, an office would be opened in a backward region and in the hilly areas even a ten per cent earning was considered sufficient. The Fifth Plan which was then in operation had set a target of establishing 31,000 new post offices in different parts of the country. By March 1977, more than 15,500 post offices had been set up in the backward and hilly areas alone. There was considerable progress in other areas under the jurisdiction of the ministry.

The Quick Mail Service (QMS) was introduced by the P&T in 1975 covering all state capitals and headquarters of all Union territories and important commercial cities and towns. The same condition that applies today for availing of this service, namely that the PIN code must be used, was made applicable when the scheme was launched under Dr. Sharma's directions. The QMS was soon extended to 45 national and 398 regional centres.

The telephone had come to India within just five years of its invention by Alexander Graham Bell. In 1976, the centenary year of the invention, the Ministry of Communications launched a scheme to instal new exchanges and add to the strength of the existing ones. Under this, 12,500 new lines were added all over the country, which, of course, in that year were inadequate to meet the growing needs of business, professional and individual subscribers.

In the area of technological improvment and upgradation, the department reached a major signpost when the country's first computerised electronic telephone exchange was set up in Delhi.

The STD (Subscriber trunk dialling) facility was introduced for the first time in 1969 between Lucknow and Kanpur. This was being gradually extended and by 1977 when Dr. Sharma ceased to be a minister as many as 241 pairs of stations were linked by STD. The ISD (international subscriber dialling) facility for calling up your friends and business associates or others abroad from your home or office was introduced during his tenure and was available between Delhi and London and Bombay and London.

The Overseas Communication Service, was, in fact, doing pretty well. In 1974-75 its total revenue was Rs. 13.89 crores. In 1976-77 it grossed Rs. 28.71 crores, more than twice its takings two years earlier. The net profit went up from Rs. 6.38 crores to Rs. 19 crores during this two year period. The Commissioning of the second satellite earth station at Dehra Dun, in addition to the first at Arvi in near Pune, was a great boost to the expansion of India's foreign telecommunication services. The Dehra Dun centre became commercially operational on December 28, 1976. It was set up with an international telecommunication exchange in Delhi and with interconnecting microwave stations in Mussoorie, Muzaffarnagar, Roorkee, Meerut and Deshgarah. The Delhi-London ISD connection owed itself to this facility being commissioned.

Speaking of the progress under the Five Year Plan, the Annual Report of the Ministry of Communications for the year 1976-77 said:[2]

"The Fifth Five Year Plan 1974-79 was finalised in September, 1976. Earlier in 1973, in the Draft Fifth Plan, a provision of Rs. 1176 crores was made for 'Communications' as against the actual expenditure of Rs. 498.56 crores during the Fourth plan period. In the final Fifth Plan, the provision for 'Communications' has been further raised to Rs. 1266.61 crores. This substantial increase in outlay on 'Communications' during the Fifth plan period has been made as it has been realised that the development of commerce and industry, in particular, and economic progress of the country including efficient administration in general depend to a very large extent on the availability of a proper communications system. It has also been appreciated that the programme for the development of communications is related to a very large extent to the timely supplies of indigenous equipment, the production of which is mainly in the public sector".

By his hard work and efficiency and with his quiet almost unobtrusive working style, Shanker Dayal achieved the same degree of rapport with his administrative and technical advisers and aides in the Ministry as he done during his years in Bhopal. The Communications Ministry is noted for the presence of a large number of highly qualified technologists and engineers and a specialised cadre of postal service officers, besides a large body of P and T and telecommunications workers who operate the various services. That not only the Minister maintained good working relations with his senior officers but industrial peace was maintained on the whole in a major department employing a large body of workers shows what quiet efficiency can achieve. Contrast it with the continued wrangles, frictions and conflicts between the political masters and the senior officers in later years.

The general organisations of the ministry is explained in the following terms:[3]

"The Ministry of Communications is headed by Secretary (Communications), who is also the Chairman, P&T Board and the Director General, Posts and Telegraphs. He is assisted by an Additional Secretary. After the introduction of the scheme of departmentalisation of accounts with effect from 1st April, 1976, Secretary (Communications) also functions as the Chief Accounting Authority in the Ministry. This responsibility is discharged by him through the Financial Adviser (Communications) and Additional Secretary, who is also Member (Finance) P&T Board, and heads the Integrated Finance Wing of the Ministry".

NOTES

1. Details of progress in P&T field taken from "India: A Reference Annual" 1975, 1976 and 1977 & 78.
2. Annual Report of the Minstry of Communications 1976-77.
3. *Ibid*.

6

ANDHRA INTERLUDE

The 1980 Lok Sabha election saw Dr. Shanker Dayal Sharma back in Parliament after a gap of three years. But he was not among the senior leaders in the Congress(I) party chosen by Mrs. Indira Gandhi to join her cabinet. There was some speculation over his non-inclusion in the Government but nobody doubted his unswerving loyalty to the party and the leader. During Indira Gandhi's years in wilderness, Shanker Dayal had stood by her from the beginning, unlike some leaders who deserted her at first but gradually went back to her.

Shanker Dayal bided his time with characteristic patience and eschewed any rancour even in private conversation with friends. This was unlike many in the party who would swear eternal loyalty to Mrs. Gandhi but lose no time in airing grievances once they were denied favours like ministerial and party appointments or fell from grade. For nearly four years Shanker Dayal did not hear any call of duty from the leader. He fulfilled his responsibilities and duties as a senior member of the party in the Lok Sabha.

The call, however, came in a most unexpected situation. In August 1984, Shanker Dayal was called upon to take over as Governor of Andhra Pradesh, one of India's bigger States. The incumbent Governor, Ram Lal, a former Chief Minister of Himachal Pradesh, had mismanaged things to an incredible extent and was virtually sacked by the Centre although for form's sack he was allowed to resign.

Andhra Pradesh was among the most loyal supporters of the Congress party and after the split in 1969 most of the top leaders of the party in the State had chosen to hitch their wagon to Mrs. Gandhi's star. The State had voted for the Congress party, now the Congress(I), election after election and gave it a higher percentage of popular vote and consequently more seats in the State assembly and the Lok Sabha, than the party had won at the national level.

The events took an anti-Congress turn in 1982-83 when a popular cinema actor, Nandamuri Taraka Rama Rao, generally known as NTR, formed a regional party called Telugu Desam, the land of the Telugus, in March 1982.[1] He toured the State and drew large crowds wherever he went, with his appeal to the "Self-respect of the Telugu People". His plea was that the Congress (I) leadership had been insulting the people of Andhra Pradesh by making and unmaking Chief Ministers in Delhi. His plea was justified in the light of the removal of Dr. Channa Reddy as Chief Minister in October 1980, just $2\frac{1}{2}$ years after he had assumed office. Channa's successor, T. Anjiah, who was a Minister of State at the Centre, was asked to go back to his State only to be replaced in February, 1982 by Bhavanam

Venkatarama Reddy. (He dropped the caste name "Reddy" after becoming Chief Minister). In between Mr. Anjiah had the distinction of having the largest cabinet in any State in the country with 61 Ministers.

NTR's attractive personality, his powerful oratory and organising skill helped him to win the January, 1983 State assembly election by a thumping majority. He had played the Telugu Self-respect card adroitly and effectively. In a reputedly Congress (I) State he won 202 seats out of 293 seats in the assembly for which elections were held (election to one seat was countermanded).

The Congress(I) rout was complete. NTR now loomed large on the national scene and hosted one of the first opposition conclaves at Vijayawada in May 1983. All the non-Congress (I) parties attended the conclave which confirmed NTR's position as a national leader. He had also had a hand in helping to organise two more conclaves, one in Delhi and the other in Srinagar.

In Andhra Pradesh itself, however, things were not going too smoothly for NTR and opposition was building up to him because of his personalised style of politics bordering on dictatorial tendencies.[2] In particular, his Finance Minister Nandedla Bhaskara Rao who had been so far a tower of strength to NTR, resented such attitude. In August 1984, NTR had gone to the United States for medical treatment and when he returned home Bhaskara Rao gave him an account of how he had been humiliated by the Chief Secretary. The Chief Minister smelt a rat and immediately had Bhaskara Rao dismissed from the cabinet. Earlier, Bhaskara Rao and three other Ministers had submitted their resignations from the cabinet but NTR preferred to sack Bhaskara Rao. That was on August 14, 1984.

Bhaskara Rao now retaliated by claiming to be the leader of a rebel Telugu Desam group and approached the

Governor claiming the support of 91 of the ruling party MLAs and some other independents and a small group. The Congress (I) also came out with a declaration of support to Bhaskara Rao. Its strength in the house was 60 members.

Governor Ram Lal dismissed NTR's Government on August 16 after giving the Telugu Desam leader an opportunity to resign and swore in Bhaskara Rao in his place. Rama Rao, however, claimed to continue to enjoy majority support in the assembly and said he was prepared to prove it in the house which he had already advised the Governor to convene on August 18. He took 171 MLAs with him to the Raj Bhavan in Hyderabad to demonstrate his strength.

Ram Lal, said to be acting on instructions from Delhi which was upset over NTR's anti-Congress(I) role at the National level, was in no mood to accommodate NTR. He refused to meet the MLAs or NTR and instead had them arrested. They were, of course, released later in the day but not before a wave of anger swept the country. Public opinion was outraged that a duly elected Government had been ousted by the Governor on the specious plea that there was a rift in the ruling Telugu Desam party and the Chief Minister had lost his majority and he was denied the opportunity to prove his majority.

Sympathy for NTR grew by the day as Bhaskara Rao made one manouevre after another to win over some of the dissatisfied Desam MLAs. On the other hand, NTR rushed to Delhi and demonstrated his strength in Rashtrapati Bhavan before President Zail Singh who was now believed to be estranged from the Prime Minister, Mrs Gandhi, and received the entire lot of NTR's MLAs. The Telugu Desam leader had a problem in keeping his flock together and away from the allurements, said to be offered for changing their loyalty, but here NTR had the support of the other opposition parties.

It was at this stage that Dr. Sharma came into the picture. Delhi had drawn enough flak from all quarters including newspapers normally friendly to the Congress (I). Ram Lal now quit his post, obviously taking the cue from the same people who in the first place had led him to the fatal course of dismissing the NTR Government. Promptly, Shanker Dayal was appointed Governor to take over at a time when the State was faced with the most unprecedented crisis.

Bhaskara Rao was busy mustering support from disgruntled Desam MLAs, not one of whom, however, stirred out of the Ramakrishna studios in Hyderabad, owned by NTR, where the MLAs were lodged. On arrival in Hyderabad, Shanker Dayal asked Bhaskara Rao to face the assembly on September 11 and prove his majority in the house. In fact, Bhaskara Rao had been asked by the previous governor also to prove his majority within a month but he had avoided calling the house into session. Shanker Dayal lost no time to put the constitutional machinery into motion and at full gear.

Bhaskara Rao was still at his game of stalling the assembly vote. He first got the Speaker, T. Satyanarayana, and Deputy Speaker, B. Reddy, both of them Telugu Desam MLAs, sworn in as ministers. The governor, therefore, appointed M. Baga Reddy, as pre-tem Speaker to conduct the proceedings of the house until a regular presiding officer was elected by the assembly. On the first day, September 11, the house was adjourned on the ground of some obituary references. Dr. Sharma told the Telugu Desam MLAs who called on him on September 12, "I am at my wits' end".[3]

Bhaskara Rao had yet another card up his sleeve. On September 13, when the house was expected to vote on a motion of confidence moved by the Chief Minister himself, Baga Reddy resigned as pre-tem Speaker. This was unheard of a pro-tem Speaker resigning. The pro-tem Speaker is there only for a brief period. Normally the senior most member of the house irrespective of the party he belongs to is appointed to the office for a couple of days.

Shanker Dayal had his answer to Bhaskara Rao's ploy. He appointed Salahuddin Owaisi, a veteran of Andhra Pradesh politics, as pro-tem Speaker and fixed September 20 as the date on which the trial of strength must take place on the floor of the house. However, things had already moved towards a climax. Bhaskara Rao had planned to storm the Ramakrishna studios and bring out the Desam MLAs in a desperate bid to cause a rift in the party and keep himself in power. Such a step, if allowed to be taken, would have had disastrous consequences.

Dr. Sharma then cut the gordian knot and dismissed Bhaskara Rao's Government on September 15 for failure of the Chief Minister to prove his majority within the stipulated period of 30 days. This was laid down by the former Governor on August 16. Simultaneously, Shanker Dayal administered the oath of office to NTR. Rama Rao was thus sworn as Chief Minister for a second time after he won a massive mandate in January, 1983.

It was obvious to the meanest intelligence that Bhaskara Rao was postponing the decision on a vote of confidence in the assembly in the hope that he would be able to win over a sufficient number of Telugu Desam MLAs. This was a mockery of the democratic process and Dr. Sharma was widely complimented for "resurrecting" democracy in Andhra Pradesh.

Here we need not go into how the wave of sympathy for NTR helped him to win both the Lok Sabha and State Assembly elections within a few months (NTR had the house dissolved and elections to a new assembly were held three years ahead of time) and how he lost the mandate in 1989-90. It is also not necessary to go into the question whether Dr. Sharma as Governor was exercising his own discretion or, as alleged by some, carrying out instructions to restore the NTR Government just as his predecessor had, on Delhi's orders, dismissed the NTR Government and thereby created a crisis.

What is relevant is the fact that in a crisis Dr. Sharma who was freshly inducted as Governor made the right decision and without losing time. The faith of the people in democracy which was rudely shaken by what had happened just 30 days ago was re-established. Dr. Sharma became instrumental in achieving that result and in burying the hatchet between Delhi and one of the major States. His personality was seen to the best advantages in a crisis situation and his faith in parliamentary democracy was well demonstrated.

Shanker Dayal was not destined to remain long in Andhra Pradesh. He was shifted to Punjab as Governor in November 1985, in the course of the Centre's policy changes in relation to the troubled State. However, Dr. Sharma's tenure in Punjab, which came to an end in March 1986, when he was transferred as Governor of Maharashtra, was a pleasant affair. The State had elections and Mr. Surjit Singh Barnala, Akali Dal (Longowal) had assumed office as Chief Minister only a couple of months earlier.

The Maharashtra tenure also came to an end a year and a half later when Dr. Sharma became India's Vice-President and shifted once again to Delhi.

A bond however grew between Shanker Dayal and the people of Andhra Pradesh. It was also during his period as Governor of the State that as a deeply religious man he was attracted to the Tirupati temple of Lord Venkateswara. From that time onwards he became a frequent visitor to Tirupati.

NOTES

1. For details of NTR's rise to power see "NTR A Biography" by S. Venkat Narayan, Vikas, 1983.
2. For further information on the crisis in Andhra Pradesh see UNI Backgrounder Vol. IX, No. 36.
3. Details of the action taken by Dr. Sharma as Andhra Pradesh Governor after arrival in Hyderabad have been taken from the *Statesman*, Delhi of the relavent dates.

7

IN THE CHAIR IN RAJYA SABHA

The Vice President of India is the ex-officio Chairman of the upper house of Parliament, the Rajya Sabha. Known as the house of elders, the Rajya Sabha has powers more or less equal to those of the popularly elected Lak Sabha, except that the Government is responsible to the Lok Sabha and a lack of majority in that house would bring it down and all financial bills, including the annual budget, must be *passed* by the Lak Sabha but only "returned" to the lower house by the Rajya Sabha.

In the earlier decades of freedom, the Rajya Sabha, known as the Council of States in the Constitution, had acquired a reputation for a less turbulent atmosphere than what prevailed in the lower house at times. The debate was marked by sobriety and decorum was maintained to a large extent. The members were often people from the professions and less involved in active politics than their counterparts in the Lok Sabha.

The picture was, however, distorted to some extent by the ruling Congress (I) and even some opposition parties making the Rajya Sabha a backdoor entry point to Parliament for some of their worthies who could not make the grade for the Lok Sabha because of their inability to win a popular election or some other reason. The practice of such persons becoming Rajya Sabha members from States other than their own also came into vogue.

As the composition of the house changed over the years the responsibilities of the presiding officer also became more and more onerous. Gone were the days when the first Vice President, the savant Dr. S. Radhakrishnan, would address the most prominent and well-liked member of the house, the late Bhupesh Gupta, of the CPI (Communist Party of India), as just "Bhupesh". He would gently but firmly ask him to sit down as Bhupesh Gupta would go on and on. The veteran communist leader had incidentally been Radhakrishnan's student in Calcutta University.

Dr. Sharma's tenure as Chairman of the Rajya Sabha from September 1987 coincided with a period of fast moving events in the political life of the country. By the time he came to occupy the chair in September 1987 the Bofors issue had surfaced and Mr. V.P. Singh and some others had left or had been expelled from the Congress (I) party. Mr. Singh, who was himself a member of the upper house then, was fast becoming the focal point of opposition unity.

In a little over two years, in the November 1989 Lok Sabha poll, the Congress (I) went out of power and V.P. Singh became Prime Minister at the head of a Janata Dal-

National Front Government, supported from the outside by the Left Front and the BJP. The Congress (I) had, however, a majority in the Rajya Sabha. A party out of power but wielding the big stick in the upper house was bound to be the cause for many unpredictable situations.

Then the Congress (I) lost its majority in the house but it was still the largest single party. (The Rajya Sabha reflects the position in the State assemblies whose members elect the Rajya Sabha.) This happened during the National Front rule and has continued even after the return of the Congress (I) to power in June 1991.

Obviously, such varying situations impose on the Chairman greater responsibilities to keep the business of the house going and maintain an even temper in the proceedings. During V.P. Singh's tenure as Prime Minister, for example, the Congress (I) members would stall the proceedings repeatedly and even prevent him from speaking. When the Congress (I) came back to power, the party sometimes got back a dose of its own medicine from the opposition.

Shanker Dayal had been elected unopposed as Vice President although he had been sponsored by the Congress (I) which was then in power at the Centre and most of the States. His Congress background was too well known to be stressed. However, from day one of his role as Chairman of the Rajya Sabha, he displayed absolute freedom from any party affiliations. This was what was expected but often there is a gap between the theoretical position and the reality.

Dr. Sharma presided over the Rajya Sabha for five years during which there were four different Prime Ministers and four different governments—Rajiv Gandhi and his Congress (I) Government, V.P. Singh and his Janata Dal-National Front Government, Chandra Shekhar and his

Janata Dal(s) Government and finally P.V. Narasimbha Rao as the head of a Congress (I) Government. Interestingly, in the lower house there were three Speakers during this period—Mr. balram Jakhar, Mr. Rabi Ray and Mr. Shivraj Patil who is the presiding officer of the tenth (present) Lok Sabha.

"Nobody could take him for granted, neither the Government nor the opposition," according to S. Jaipal Reddy, a prominent member of the Rajya Sabha. "He was absolutely fair, in the house and in the Business Advisory Committee (BAC)"[1] The BAC, on which the parties are represented in proportion to their strength in the house, takes major decisions on the time to be allotted for different debates and other business of the house.

Jaipal Reddy was member of the eighth Lok Sabha (1985–89) and then moved to the Rajya Sabha, first as a front bench member of the ruling Janata Dal, and then as Leader of the Opposition in the upper house for nearly a year. In July 1992 he became leader of the Janata Dal group in the house after he ceased to be the leader of the opposition. He has had ample opportunities to watch Dr. Sharma from a distance as well as from close quarters.

Reddy was particularly happy about the conduct of the question hour business, the first hour each day when members put questions and ministers (including the Prime Minister) answer them. "Dr. Sharma gave maximum satisfaction to members and more questions could be covered. The way he explained the questions to the ministers and interpreted the answers to the members was remarkable. Before he came to the house he would have studied both the questions and their answers. He was always alert during the question hour. Dr. Sharma would not hesitate to pull up a minister for an inadequate answer or a member for putting an irrelevant question or supplementary."

It was not, however, the question hour alone which marked Dr. Sharma's emphatic role. Although he generally did not stay in the house after the question hour was over, he would take decisions marked by fairness, impartiality and transparency, on the "Zero Hour" business, the issues sought to be raised by members on matters of urgent importance by way of special mention, said Jaipal Reddy. The decisions would be conveyed to the members and the Deputy Chairman or whoever took the chair afterwards.

It was one of these decisions on a special mention over which serious trouble arose in the house in 1988 when the Congress (I) had a big presence in the house and even Prime Minister Rajiv Gandhi was present. It was the first day of the budget session, February 23, 1988, and after the question hour was over P. Upendra, then leader of the Telugu Desam group, rose to make a special mention on the expenditure incurred by the Andhra Pradesh Governor, Miss Kumudben Joshi, in excess of the norms prescribed for Governors by the Home Ministry.

Upendra was then an upcoming leader of the opposition and when the V.P. Singh Government came to power in December 1989 he became Minister of Information and Broadcasting and Parliamentary Affairs. Interestingly, he has been expelled from the Telugu Desam party now and he is an unattached member of the Rajya Sabha.

Dr. Sharma who had permitted Upendra to make a special mention on the Governor's action was also in the chair on that day when the Telugu Desam leader got up to speak. Promptly a number of Congress (I) MPs and even ministers rose to object to the Chairman's action and said the Governor's actions could not be discussed.

Dr. Sharma stood by his decision and said Upendra would not be permitted to cast espersions on the Governor or her conduct but at a time when there was a severe drought in the country (the 1987-88 drought) the question of controlling expenditure could be discussed.[2] There was uproar in the house as more and more ruling party members and some ministers criticised the Chairman's ruling while the numerically weak opposition stood by the ruling and Upendra's right to make his special mention.

Tempers rose and two ministers, P. Chidambaram, Minister of State for Internal Security, considered close to Rajiv Gandhi, and Minister of State for Surface Transport Rajesh Pilot—both of whom significantly were not members of the Rajya Sabha—were prominent in objecting to the Chairman's action. Obviously pressure was being put on the Vice President by the ruling party to reverse his decision.

Shanker Dayal pleaded with them and argued it was his ruling and they could not question it. He repeatedly said "Will you hear me?" "Kindly hear me". He told the ruling party that they were giving an impression as though they had something to hide.

As a senior journalist observed[3], "Such a thing had never happened before in the 38 years history of the Indian Parliament—the way the ruling party seniors, Ministers included, challenged the Vice President and Rajya Sabha Chairman Dr. Shanker Dayal Sharma..." When Dr Sharma found things going beyond all reasonable limits and the defiance by the ruling party (which had in the first place put him in the chair) amounted to a challenge to his authority he told the Treasury Benches and the two ministers: "My advice to Mr. Chidambaram and Mr. Pilot is, you do not have to do anything more. You decide it in your party and if you decide that I should go out I will go out. If the Congress Party, the ruling party, decides that I am not fit to occupy the chair, I will go out You can go and discuss it with your leader."[4]

Rajiv Gandhi, who was present in the house when the trouble began and while the tumult rose, had left the house at a later stage and was not present there when these remarks were made. His partymen, however, did not allow the ruling to be enforced and Upendra withdrew his special mention. The opposition pleaded with Dr. Sharma not to think of quitting.

Of course, there was no serious move in that direction, although the air was thick with rumours of the Vice President's resignation. The matter seems to have been discussed privately between the Vice President and the Prime Minister and the latter made amends for the events of February 23. Not before, however, senior partymen like P. Shiv Shanker, leader of the house and a minister in the Rajiv Cabinet, and N.K. P. Salve had gone before the Press and sought to justify the action of their party members.

But veteran Congress (I) leader, Kamalapati Tripathi, congratulated Dr. Sharma on "taking a correct stand" and behaving like "a true Congressman."

The ugly happenings, however, did not dampen Shanker Dayal's spirits and his attitude of upholding the traditions of free discussion and maintaining the decorum of the house did not suffer any change. He did not put any curbs on the members, whether they belonged to the ruling party or one of the opposition groups, provided the rules of the house and its conventions permitted them to raise the issues they sought to bring up.

But controversy cropped up once again in a big way more than two years later when a former Congress (I) minister, K.K. Tewary, made a vicious attack on Dr. Sharma. In May 1990, Dr. Sharma had occasion to pull up the Congress (I) party members in the house, then in the opposition, for their unruly behaviour and for rushing into the well of the house (the area separating the chair from the members). He had uttered a few words of admonition which he would have done whatever the party affiliation of the offending members.

The next day[5], the house was agitated when it was pointed out by some members that a statement by K.K. Tewary had appeared in some papers, one of which had given the full text, in which the former Union Minister of State for External Affairs and Information and Broadcasting, had used the most objectionable phrases of abuse against the Vice President. Tewary went to the extent of saying that Dr. Sharma was not fit to preside over the Rajya Sabha. His Statement described Dr. Sharma's remarks "the most vitriolic and undignified denunciation of Congress members" which Shanker Dayal had allowed to stay on record. He used words like "hysterical rantings" for Shanker Dayal's words and "simulated dramatics" for his action for breaking down in the house, forgetting that despite his years of political experiences and great maturity Dr. Sharma is an emotional person.

With Shanker Dayal scrupulously keeping aloof from the controversy the house took up Tewary's challenge and the sternnest action was demanded against him. The Deputy Chairperson, Mrs. Najma Heptullah, was in the chair. His own party was terribly embarrassed by his statement. The party has no intention to defend his indefensible position nor did it went to be isolated in the house over the demand for action against the offending former minister, but at the same time the party leaders did not like to appear to be letting down a former minister. That was at least the impression gained when the first reaction of the party seniors like P. Shiv Shanker and N.K.P. Salve was noted.

Shiv Shanker, by then leader of the opposition, offered to apologise on behalf of Tewary for his demaging remarks against the Chairman but the house would have none of it. Salve said Tewary should not be condemned without being given a chance to defend himself. He was reacting to the proposal that Tewary be issued a notice to clarify whether the statement in the press was genuine and if so he should appear at the bar of the house to be reprimanded.

Ultimately, Shiv Shanker and Finance Minister Madhu Dandavate prepared a draft which incorporated the same points. The motion was moved by P. Upendra, Minister of Parliamentary Affairs, and seconded by Shiv Shankar. A notice was served on Tewary to say whether it was his statement that had appeared in the press and if so face the music, namely, be prepared to be reprimanded. The house did not see any scope for defence once the offending party admitted the statement was his own.

Tewary tried to take recourse to judicial process and approached the Supreme Court but the highest judicial body refused to be drawn into the controversy.[6] It dismissed Tewary's writ petition saying Parliament was fully empowered to take a decision on a breach of its privilege.

All the while Dr. Sharma stayed away from the goings on inside the house or outside it. He was not present in the house when the issue was taken up on May 24 and a notice was sent to Tewary. Neither did he make any effort to influence the course that the controversy was taking. As Jaipal Reddy put it, "Not only did Dr. Sharma keep his cool but he also maintained a transcendental distance from the developments."[7]

The house was, however, too perturbed by Tewary's blatant statement and in a rare display of unanimity the motion serving a notice was adopted by the entire House.

By now the Congress (I) party had also realised that it must distance itself from Tewary and a showcause notice was issued to him by the AICC(I) asking him why he should not be expelled from the party. (Finally, however, this was not followed up.)

Turned away by the Supreme Court and denounced by his own party, Tewary offered to apologies but this was not acceptable to the house. He finally appeared at the bar of the house on June 1, 1991 to be openly reprimanded for his "grave misdemeanour". Deputy Chairman Heptullah, after ascertaining from the deputy director of security whether the "contemner" was present, administered the reprimand with almost the full house in attendance, the various galeries full and Tewary silently listening to the statement of his reprimand:[8]

"K.K. Tewary, this House has deplored the grave act of misdemeanour for which you bear responsibility in committing contempt of this House. The House is pained that a citizen of India should ever have been so at fault and apparently be unrepentant thereafter. This house, therefore, reprimands you and more severe penalty is not administered only in the hope that through introspection would realise the seriousness of your misdemeanour towards this House and to the sacred system of Parliamentary democracy."

This was perhaps the first case of anyone being called to the bar of the Rajya Sabha and being reprimanded. In the Lok Sabha there was a similar instance when the editor of a Bombay weekly was reprimanded for insulting Acharya Kripalani, then a member of the House. Jawaharlal Nehru was the Prime Minister.

Dr. Sharma had unintentionally made history. Left to himself he would have perhaps forgiven Tewary although the latter had, as noted by the Rajya Sabha, been quite unrepentant.

Jaipal Reddy also recalls how Shanker Dayal was not too hidebound to be a slave to rules and precedents if something required to be done like when Reddy, as Leader of the Opposition, wanted to authenticate and lay on the table some documents, concerning correspondence between the Finance ministry and the World Bank in the autumn session of Parliament in 1991. Reddy said this was a recognised practice in the Lok Sabha and documents were allowed to be tabled after being authenticated by a member if the Speaker permitted it. But in the Rajya Sabha the procedure was unknown and the Chairman was told so. But he finally permitted Jaipal Reddy to authenticate and table the documents which the Government itself then realised must be placed before the House.[9] Precedents are generally followed. Here a precedent was set.

Dr. Sharma took the business of Parliament seriously and one cannot do better than recall what he had said about Nehru in a tribute to the first Prime Minister's high regard for Parliamentary Democracy, Parliament and its daily routine.

In his Pannalal Saraogi Memorial lecture organised by the Ramakrishna Mission Institute of Culture, Calcutta on April 30, 1989, Dr. Sharma observed:[10]

"Almost twentyfive years have gone by since he(Nehru) left us. In the interim a vast mass of data has accumulated about Panditji's normative leadership in the first two decades of Parliamentary Democracy. In our country .... Jawaharlal Nehru, by his approach and actions, created an ideal for the functioning of the system. ...Elections are basic to democracy... "He had said : 'Democracy is based on the active and intelligent interest of the people in their national affairs and in the elections that result in the formation of Government. The fact that one party happens to be in charge of Government does not entitle it to any privilege during elections ....Officers of the Government must function impartially... The Ministers of the Government must not utilise their official position to further their own election prospects in any way... Our propaganda by speech or in writing should not be personal but should deal with policies and programmes...'"

Nehru, as quoted by Sharma, thus goes on to give what we may call today the 'do's and don'ts' of elections but which most parties honour in their breach. Sharma says : "Ethical and moral values reigned supreme with him. ...In deciding the selection of Congress candidates in elections, Panditji placed the highest importance on the integrity and reputation of the person." Not on his winning capability, we may add for the benefit of the people who now decide or report in the media on such things. Sharma goes on :

".....Yet Panditji, ever the true democrat, was unfailing in his respect for the will of the people. A telling illustration is his position on the linguistic states." Shanker Dayal recalls Nehru's aversion to linguistic states but how finally "he bowed to the intense public mood in a number of states in favour of a linguistic re-configuration of state boundaries."

Analysing Nehru's role as a democrat wedded to the Parliamentary form, Sharma adds : "The cabinet form of Government and the doctrine of ministerial responsibility provides another telling illustration of Panditji's nurturing of an important feature of Parliamentary democracy.... The support of the masses, and not merely the powers that went with the office of Prime Minister gave him weight in the cabinet. After Sardar Patel's passing away, Nehru towered over his colleagues in the Government... Yet Jawaharlal Nehru did not dominate or seek to dominate members of his cabinet... The regularity, timeliness and thoroughness of cabinet meetings, Jawaharlalji's crisp and incisive summing up of discussions... all these made for uniquely efficient discharge of business by the Council of Ministers."[11]

"But, above all," says Sharma, "Jawaharlal Nehru recognised and daily nurtured the importance of Parliament, the scope, powers and privileges of Parliament, the position and dignity of the presiding officers and its proceedings, rules and conventions. It was Panditji's role within the Lok Sabha and the Rajya Sabha, and relative to its officers and procedures and proceedings that contributed so basically to the consolidation and growth of Parliamentary Democracy in India....Nehru throughout his seventeen years as Prime Minister enriched the ethos of Parliamentary Democracy in India by his exemplary attitude towards matters pertaining to Parliament. ... As Prime Minister, Panditji by the force of his personality and personal commitment, ensured that Government remained truly responsible to Parliament."

Dr. Sharma also recalls the incident in the Rajya Sabha in the last days of Nehru when Nehru who was "ill, mortally ill",, insisted on rising to answer questions or make interventions and declined the request of the Chairman, Dr Zakir Hussain, to speak while seated. "Each time, despite the pain, he (Nehru) struggled to force himself to his legs and only then did he speak.".

The date of the Pannalal Saraogi lecture was April 30, 1989, more than a year after the incident of February 23, 1988, narrated in some detail in this chapter.

NOTES

1. S. Jaipal Reddy in personal communication to the author.

2. For details of the February 23, 1988 incident *Frontline* Madras, March 5-18, 1988 issue relied upon.
3. K.K.Katyal in *Frontline* Op.Cit.
4. As quoted in *Frontline.*
5. National Herald, Delhi May 25, 1990
6. *Frontline, Sunday,* Calcutta, and several other news sources of the relevant period consulted.
7. In personal communication to the author.
8. The *Statesman,* Delhi, June 2, 1990
9. Reddy in personal communication to the author.
10. *Ibid.*
11. See *Jawaharlal Nehru,* by S.D. Sharma, Sterling, Delhi, 1989, chapter 4, "Jawaharlal Nehru and Parliamentary Democracy".

The voting strength of the ballets cast by the MPs taken together is equivalent to the total votes of the all the assembly members.

The fact that the President has the power to appoint the Prime Minister becomes crucial in a situation in which the Lok Sabha election does not throw up a party with a clear majority. In December 1989, President Venkataraman called upon the Janata Dal leader, Mr. V.P. Singh, to form a Government although his party did not command a clear majority in the lower house. His Government, however, had the support of the Left Front and the BJP and together the three-the Janata Dal or the National Front, of which the Dal was the biggest component, the LF and the BJP- constituted a majority of the house. Likewise, in November 1990 when the V.P. Singh Government fell after the BJP withdrew support, Mr. Venkataraman decided to invite Mr. Chandra Shekhar, leader of the breakaway Janata Dal(S), to form a Government even though he had the support of around 50 members only in the Lok Sabha. He, however, had been promised support by Rajiv Gandhi, leader of the Congress(I), although the support was virtually withdrawn after just four months.

After Chandra Shekhar thus lost majority support in the Lok Sabha and could not present the budget for 1991-92, the President dissolved the Lok Sabha and ordered fresh elections. This power to dissolve the house, exercised by the President in an unusual situation, again makes the position of the President one of high significance. Besides, the President has to interact continually with the Prime Minister and the relationship has to be one free from friction, although on several occasions this happy augury has been conspicuous by its absence.

Going back to the time when the Janata party Government of Morarji Desai fell in July 1979, one may recall that the President, Neelam Sanjiva Reddy, had sworn in Chaudhuri Charan Singh on the promise of support by Mrs Indira Gandhi, leader of the Congress(I). The support was withdrawn even before the Chaudhuri could prove his majority in the house. The next thing Reddy did was to dissolve the Lok Sabha without exploring the possibility of forming an alternative Government while the Charan Singh Government remained in office.

No wonder the ruling party wants as President a person of its choice. At the same time the President has to be an individual of high standing and one who could lend dignity to the highest office in the country.

The political scene in May-June 1992 was agog with moves and countermoves by the leading political parties and leaders on the choice of a presidential candidate. The Congress(I) being in a minority in Parliament as well as in the total electoral college in the country was genuinely in need of support from some major opposition group if it wanted to be sure of getting its candidate elected. Mr. P.V. Narasimha Rao, Prime Minister and President of the ruling Congress(I) party, had consultations with leaders of the opposition parties in search of what the party fondly calls a "consensus".

No consensus could, however, be reached. For one thing the party did not try for a genuine consensus which really means that a solution or proposition acceptable to a large majority is arrived at through the process of discussion and consultation. A consensus is not a preconceived solution, suitable to a dominant minority, which is imposed on the others in the name of arriving at a "consensus". In the case of the presidential candidate, Narasimha Rao's discussions did not really amount to an effort to focus on a single personality like Shanker Dayal Sharma.

Secondly, before the issue could reach a definite stage, the scheduled caste and scheduled tribe (SC/ST) leaders were in the field demanding that a candidate from either of the two sections be nominated for the election to the office of President. Considerable weight was lent to their voice when Janata Dal leader and former Prime Minister V. P. Singh came out in open support of the demand. He even threatened to resign from the Lok Sabha if he was thwarted by his party from pursuing this end.

But the Congress(I) party it was which fired the first shot on June 18 when it announced that Dr. Sharma, Vice President of India, would be the party's candidate for the office of President and sought other parties support.[2] Before that Narasimha Rao had called on Sharma and obtained his consent. For the Congress(I) this was the obvious thing to do since Sharma had been one of the pillars of the party at a time when it had faced a difficult situation, like the time of the 1969 split and immediately thereafter, and served the nation in different capacities including Vice President in the immediately preceding five years (frcm September 4, 1987). Since becoming Vice President Sharma had ceased to be a party man. He was besides a person of unimpeachable character and one of the few public men in the land who had no skeletons in the cupboard.

As party President Rao had beeıı authorised by the Congress(I) Working Committee to choose a presidential candidate. His critics hinted that he had chosen Sharma because he wanted a northerner to ride along with him in the mostly decorative office of head of State.[3] His motive, they said, was to close the options of his rivals in the party, who are said to be northerners, in any likely tussle for party leadership which could threaten his own position.

Whatever his motivation, Rao could have secured widespread support for Sharma and obtained a real "consensus", if he had tried for one. He was criticised by the National Front and the Bharatiya Janata Party(BJP) for not bringing about a consensus. He denied it. At his press conference on June 30, Rao was asked about it and his reply was:

"In the case of the candidature of the President and Vice President I did consult all parties, leaders. There is no question of taking any unilateral decision, I mean in the sense that I came to a conclusion without asking anyone or without consulting anyone."[4]

There was no doubt that Dr Sharma's nomination would receive a wide measure of support. Even those who were interested in putting up a candidate to oppose him never uttered a word against him. His own reaction to his nomination was brief and typically restrained. He said: "I have heard the decision just now. I am touched by the confidence reposed in me"[5].

A large number of people rushed to the Vice President's house to congratulate him and wish him success. They were received with warmth and sweets but there were no exultations. In Bhopal, where he was born and in whose service he had worked for years, jubilation was reported.[6]

"The right man for the right job", said a senior writer in the *Hindustan Times.*[7] The *Tribune* of Chandigarh in an editorial, "Obvious Choice" said[8]: "It is true the Congress party has nominated him (Dr Sharma) for the presidentship, but nobody has as yet said he has any serious objection to Dr Sharma's candidature". The paper asked the Prime Minister to continue to strive for a consensus and observed: "It would ... be in the fitness of things if Dr. Sharma were to be elected unopposed."

Similar sentiments were voiced by several other leading dailies in different languages but a contest was inevitable for the reason that the Janata Dal was now committed to an SC/ST candidate and the BJP, which had been a tacit supporter of the minority Government of Narasimha Rao for nearly a year without claiming to do so, was now openly opposed to it and was not losing any opportunity to demonstrate its opposition. The Left Front was keen that Narasimha Rao make a package announcement, on both the President and Vice President, but the West Bengal Chief Minister and prominent Communist Party of India Marxist (CPIM) leader came out in support of Dr Sharma's candidature even before his party's politburo met formally to endorse it.

The CPIM's official announcement of support came on June 23 after the National Front and Left Front failed in their joint deliberations to agree on a common candidate for the President's office. The National Front opted for Professor G. G. Swell from Meghalaya, a former Deputy Speaker of the Lok Sabha, because of his being to a Scheduled Tribe leader while the CPIM made it clear it wanted a SC/ST personality for the office of Vice President but did not wish the presidential election to become a subject of controversy and a continuation of its opposition to the Congress Government's policies.

The CPIM statement said it was supporting Dr. Sharma's candidature taking into account "the prevailing situation in the country and the necessity to have a person with appropriate stature as President who will uphold the democratic and secular values embodied in the Constitution."[9] Here the party hinted at the fact that the BJP has had also come out in support of Prof. Swell and this, in its view, vitiated the situation as it would not like to be associated with the BJP in a co-ordinated effort to fight for a candidate.

The CPI, another major segment of the Left Front, took considerably longer to announce its decision. It announced its support for Dr. Sharma on June 28, Nominations were filed for Dr. Sharma and Prof. Swell and an independent candidate, lawyer Ram Jethmalani, MP, who stood as an independent candidate but retired from the contest in favour of Swell, and a fourth candidate not considered a serious contender.

The Forward Bloc, another Left Front constituent, came out in support of Dr. Sharma soon after the CPI had done it but the Revolutionary Socialist Party, RSP, had already announced its decision to stay away from the fray. Chandra Shekhar's Party, the Samajwadi Janata Party, said it would support Dr. Sharma, thus leaving the BJP and the National Front, (minus its small constituent, the Congress(S), which said it would support Sharma) as the main supporters of Prof. Swell.

Both Sharma and Swell did not undertake any campaign in support of their candidature, unlike some candidates in the past contests who had visited almost every state to meet the MLAs and the local MPs. There was, however, a difference; while Swell held a press conference and gave interviews to the media pleading for support for himself, Dr. Sharma stayed put in his 6 Maulana Azad road house. He would neither campaign nor even privately ask for the MPs' and MLAs' votes. No interviews, no press statements.

With an elightened electorate constituting the electoral college for the office of President, a campaign was really not needed. Besides, there was continuous coverage of the forthcoming contest in the daily and weekly press and the goings on in the political parties, including the controversy over a "conscience" vote in the Janata Dal, kept on reminding the electors of the crucial vote on July 13.

NOTES

1. Article 74, substituted by an amendment of the Constitution by the Congress(I) in 1976, reads:

   "There shall be a council of ministers with the Prime Minister at the head to aid and advise the President who shall in exercise of his functions act in accordance with such advice".

   By a proviso, added in 1979 when the Janata party was in power, it was made clear that the President could ask the Council of Ministers to reconsider its advice but after doing so once the advice of the Council of Ministers is binding on the President.

2. See *Business and Political Observer*, June 22, 1992 "S.D. Sharma - Impeccable credentials for the top post" by Rajiv Shukla.

3. *Indian Express* June 19, 1992 "Cong Names Sharma for Presidential Poll".

4. Transcript of PM's Press Conference, pp.10-11, released by Press Information Bureau, New Delhi.

5. *Hindustan Times*, June 19, 1992.

6. *Hindustan Times*, June 20, 1992.

7. *Hindustan Times*, June 22, 1992.

8. *Tribune*, June 21, 1992.

9. *The Times of India*, June 24, 1992

9

AND THE RESULT

Dr. Sharma's victory in the presidential election was a foregone conclusion, going by the logic of numbers, after the parties came out with their decisions on the candidate they would support in the poll. The Congress(I) which had sponsored Shanker Dayal as its candidate and the Communist Party of India Marxist (CPIM), which was the first major party to announce support for him, together constituted a majority in the electoral college. When the Communist Party of India (CPI) also came out in support of Dr. Sharma and a number of smaller parties followed suit the numbers game was already won by him.

The candidature of Prof. G.G. Swell, sponsored by the Bharatiya Janata Party (BJP) and the National Front (NF), without any co-ordination between them, had also the support of some minor groups. He was thus assured of a little over one-third of the total votes which left him much behind in the contest. Prof. Swell had given a number of interviews and met the press in Delhi, although Dr Sharma had scrupulously kept aloof from the contest.

The Congress(I) had, however, not taken any chances and pressed senior party leaders into service to ensure that there was no cross voting by their members in favour of the opposition candidate, either in Delhi or the States. Strong teams of ministers and party functionaries were deputed to the State capitals to keep in touch with the voters, the MLAs and such MPs who had opted to cast their votes in their home States.

Precautions of this nature are justified because temptations sometimes lead members of a party to exercise their franchise in favour of the rival in violation of the party directive. This has often happened in the elections to the Rajya Sabha in which the members of a State assembly are the electors. Large sum of money are said to change hands and other favours are distributed to ensure the victory of a candidate who might have been assured of some votes but might lack the requisite number.

In the context of the present presidential context, in which Swell had been sponsored by the BJP and the NF specially on the ground that he was a Scheduled Tribe member, the Congress(I) wanted to guard against some of its scheduled caste and scheduled tribe members going against the party mandate and favouring a candidate who was from their rank. Just on the eve of the contest the Forum of SC and ST members of Parliament and State assemblies had met in Delhi and asked for the president to be chosen from one of the two sections of society, the Scheduled Castes and Scheduled Tribes.

As it turned out, the Congress(I) precautions did not seem to be called for. Not only the Congress(I) members in

Parliament and the assemblies voted for Dr. Sharma and there was no cross voting from the Congress(I) to the opposite side, but there was actually some cross voting from the other side in favour of Dr. Sharma.

The Returning Officer for the poll, Mr. Sudarshan Agarwal, Secretary General of the Rajya Sabha, declared Dr. Sharma elected as the ninth President of India at the end of the counting of votes on July 16, 1992, just a few moments before 6 p.m. This enabled the 1800 hours news bulletin of All India Radio to bring the result to the people all over the country. The counting was done in Parliament House in New Delhi. Ballet boxes from the State capitals had been flown into Delhi after the voting took place on July 13 simultaneously in Delhi and the State capitals. The members of the two houses of Parliament and the State assemblies are the voters in the presidential contest.

Dr. Sharma won by a big margin. He polled 64.78 per cent votes while Swell secured 33.21 per cent of the total valid votes. In actual terms, Sharma polled 6,75,864 value votes as against his rival who got votes valued at 3,46,485. Prof. Swell's votes were slightly below the expectations based on the actual strength of the parties sponsoring and supporting him, the gap being 1.5 per cent.

Although the lawyer, Mr Ram Jethmalani, had announced that he had withdrawn from the contest in favour of Prof. Swell, votes valued at 2,704 were cast in his favour by his admirers. Even Kaka Joginder Singh, *alias* Dhartipakad, did not lack admirers. He also polled a nominal 1,135 votes, by an MP and three MLAs who chose him as their candidate.

By and large the voting was on expected lines. But at many places there was a marginal or small cross voting in Sharma's favour which pushed up his score above the expected 60 per cent. In Bihar State only Swell got more votes than the total strength commanded by the Janata Dal and its allies and the BJP. In West Bengal, Tripura, Arunachal Pradesh and Sikkim, the entire vote was in favour of Shanker Dayal. Swell got much less support than did Sharma in the north-eastern States, including Swell's home State of Meghalaya. For that matter, Sharma polled only 65 votes in Madhya Pradesh, his home State, as against 235 for his rival in this BJP-ruled State.

The voting pattern is now only of academic interest. The important point to be noted is that if a consensus had been sought and achieved, which was quite possible considering that Dr. Sharma was widely acceptable, Dr. Sharma's victory would have been even more noteworthy. Prof. Swell who had the support of two major parties, the Janata Dal and its National Front allies and the BJP, succeeded in securing a higher percentage of votes than any secured by an opposition candidate except in the 1967 presidential poll when Dr. Ram Manohar Lohia had successfully wielded all non-Congress parties into a single whole. The following figures are relevant:

The percentage of votes polled by the winning candidate in presidential elections:

Margin of Victory

		Votes Value	Percentage
1.	Dr. Rajendra Prasad (May 3, 1952)	507.400	83.8
2.	Dr. Rajendra Prasad (May 6, 1957)	459,698	99.3
3.	Dr. S. Radhakrishnan (May 7, 1962)	553,067	98.3
4.	Dr. Zakir Hussain (May 6, 1967)	471,244	56.2

		Votes Value	Percentage
5.	V.V.Giri (August 16, 1969)	420,077	50.2
6.	Fakhruddin Ali Ahmed (August 17, 1974)	765,58	80.2
7.	Neelam Sanjiva Reddy (August 6, 1977)	Unoppose	
8.	Zail Singh (July 12, 1982)	754,113	72.7
9.	Ramaswamy Venkataraman (July, 1987)	740,198	72.3
10.	Dr. S.D. Sharma (July 16, 1992)	675,864	64.78

All rivalry was forgotten as Prof. Swell went to the 6, Maulana Azad road residence of the Vice-President of India soon after the result was announced on July 16. He congratulated Dr. Sharma and called him "my friend". They embraced each other. Dr. Sharma was the recipient of congratulations from all quarters and all sections of the people who lined up for being received by the President-elect for days together after the result was announced.

On July 16, the Prime Minister, Mr P.V. Narasimha Rao, was among the first to call on Dr. Sharma and his wife, Vimla Sharma. Asked by newsmen Mr. Rao said: "The country has got the right President, most capable, and the country's future is safe in his hands."

The winner was full of modesty in his reactions to the historic triumph. Shanker Dayal said he was conscious of a sense of deep humility and profound gratitude at the confidence expressed in him by legislators and parliamentarians of diverse political parties.

He continued, "I am aware of the honour that has been done to me and equally the responsibility that I shall have to shoulder". He hoped that the Almighty would "give me the strength to fulfil the role of constitutional head of the country by rendering devoted service in keeping with the ideals held aloft by the Father of the Nation, Mahatma Gandhi, and the great leaders of our struggle for freedom and national reconstruction."

Like every other citizen, Dr. Sharma said, he hoped to see India a land of peace, harmony and prosperity and social justice, making her own rightful contribution to the building of a better future for all humankind. "He also said that the presidential contest had been entered into by all concerned in the proper spirit and it signified the quality of India's time tested system of Parliamentary Democracy. That he should mention Parliamentary Democracy in his victory message was significant.

Mrs. Vimla Sharma, his wife, expressed gratitude to God for her husband's elevation to the highest office in the country and said that she prayed that during his tenure the nation would progress towards prosperity and happiness in an atmosphere of peace and national unity. On her own role as the First Lady, Mrs. Vimla Sharma said: "In my own capacity I will try to preserve the tradition of an Indian wife and work for the progress of the women of India."

The following table gives the detailed result:

President election results—1992

State/	No. of Value		Votes Polled								Invalid		Total		Valid
Parliament	MPs/	of each	S.D. Sharma		G.G.Swell		Dhartipakad		R. Jethmalani						Votes
	MLAs	Vote	Votes	Value	Votes	Value	Votes	Value	Votes	Value	Votes	Value	Votes	Value	(Value)
Andhra Pradesh	294	148	204	30192	73	10804					8	1184	285	42180	40996
Arunachal Pradesh	60	8	60	480									60	480	480
Assam	126	116	99	11484	19	2204			1	116	5	580	124	14384	13804
Bihar	324	174	126	21924	172	29928	1	174			1	174	300	52200	52026
Goa	40	20	27	540	11	220			1	20	1	20	40	800	780
Gujarat	182	147	105	15435	66	9702			1	147	3	441	175	25725	25284
Haryana	90	112	72	8064	17	1904			1	112			90	10080	10080
Himachal Pradesh	68	51	19	969	46	2346					2	102	67	3417	3315
Karnataka	224	131	197	25807	22	2882					5	655	224	29344	28689
Kerala	140	152	132	20064	2	304			2	304			136	20672	20672
Madhya Pradesh	320	130	65	8450	235	30550	1	130	1	130	7	910	309	40170	29260
Maharashtra	288	175	223	39025	53	9275					1	175	277	48475	48300

Manipur	60	18	56	1008	3	54			1	18			60	1080	1080
Meghalaya	60	17	36	612	23	391							59	1003	1003
Mizoram	40	8	26	208	13	104							39	312	312
Orissa	147	149	23	3427	119	17731					2	298	144	21456	21158
Punjab	177	116	97	11252	15	1740			1	116	3	348	166	13456	13108
Rajasthan	200	129	84	10836	110	14190	1	129	1	129	3	387	199	25671	25284
Sikkim	32	7	32	224									32	224	224
Tamil Nadu	234	176	228	40128	5	880							233	41008	41008
Tripura	60	26	53	1378									53	1378	1378
Uttar Pradesh	425	208	128	26624	280	58240			1	208	5	1040	414	86112	85072
West Bengal	294	151	263	39713							7	1057	270	40770	39713
Parliament	776	702	510	358020	218	153036	1	702	2	1404	14	9828	745	522990	513162
Grand Total	4601		2865	675864	1502	346485	4	1135	13	2704	67	17199	4451	1043387	1026188
Percentage				64.78%		33.21%		0.11%		0.26%		1.65%			
Lead				329379									NIC/	RSS	

10

VALUES AND BELIEFS

As a self-effacing person Shanker Dayal has made no conscious effort to cultivate the media. Consequently, not much of significance has been written about him, specially about his thinking, his approach to life and on what lines the nation should, in his opinion, base itself so as to be able to march forward. His speeches, however, reveal the man as nothing else does. They reflect his thoughts and show how deeply he is concerned about the basic features of life in India. They also show he has well thought out objectives to set before the people.

With his urge to learn from the great men of India, he spoke again and again of the deep debt under which these men had laid the nation with their contribution in various fields of human endeavour. In his books *Eminent Indians,*[1] with its Hindi counterpart *Deshamani*[2], along with its companion volume *Hamare Path-Pradarshak*[3], he has put together the rich tributes he paid to more than 50 of them, drawn from diverse fields. Among them are to be found Mahatma Gandhi and Jawaharlal Nehru, Maulana Azad and Acharya Narendra Deva, Jayaprakash Narayan and Bhimrao Ambedkar, literary and religious leaders like Amir Khushro, Dayanand Saraswati, Allama Iqbal and Makhanlal Chaturvedi.

Interestingly, even a modest person reveals himself when he speaks of the greatness of others because the qualities and attributes he singles out for commendation are often the qualities he admires and stands for. His own value system can be discerned in such speeches.

Not only in the tributes Shanker Dayal has paid to those great sons of India but also in his analytical and detailed accounts, enriched with apt quotations and references from religious, literary, historical and other works, which we come across in other books of his speeches - *Jawaharlal Nehru* and *Horizons of Indian Education*[4] - we can look for and find the basic values cherished by Dr. Sharma.

He is never tired of speaking of the greatness of India and of her proud cultural heritage. But he warns us not take a narrow view of India and her heritage. He tells the people to absorb the good points of others and keep their mental horizon wide and open. In his convocation address to the Sri Sathya Sai Institute of Higher learning, Puthaparty, in Andhra Pradesh, which is a deemed university, Dr. Sharma spoke extensively on this theme. He said:

"Our Indian tradition is not an ostrich-like attitude refusing to see and absorb the light of learning around us from different parts of the world. The whole world is a family, *"Vasudhaiva Kutumbakam"* is our ideal. In the words of Adi Sankara, *"Swadesho Bhuvanatrayam"* - all the three worlds are our "motherland". At the same time, the acid test of rational discrimination of what is right and what is wrong should be applied, or in other words, the students ought to learn it from the master, how to apply it...."[5] He then goes on to quote the great Sanskrit poet Kalidasa and says according to the poet "all that is old is not gold and all that is mod is not bad."[6]

In the same address, Dr. Sharma recalled the great scientific and other contributions made by India to the world, which have advanced the cause of science, philosophy and the fine arts in the world. He said : "The whole world knows the Indian origin of the fundamentals of modern sciences. The so-called Arabic numerals are called Hindsa in Arabic itself, meaning "from India". The concept of the zero and the decimal system are traced to Indian thought. Ancient India produced the most valuable treatises on astronomy, mathematics, cosmology, geography, physiology, and medicine, logic and philosophy, sculpture and architecture, music and dance, on grammer, prosody and linguistics, as well as the science of war including the training of elephants and horses."[7]

But he warned the people against becoming inward-looking. "There is an increasing tendency on our part to boast of this past. Such ignorant pride does not lead us anywhere; that is why we should remind ourselves of the Vedic maxim "*Aa no Bhadra Kratavo Yantu Vishwatah* - let noble thoughts come to us from all sides". We should freely and frankly accept the thoughts of all countries and of all languages. Mahatma Gandhi told us to keep the windows of our home open to the winds of all countries but we should be careful that we are not swept off our feet. He thus emphasised the basic Indianness of our education."[8]

Shanker Dayal may be modest in his approach and under- statement rather than emphatic assertion may be his preference when it comes to propounding a view. But he does not hesitate in stating his views even when they may run counter to the fashionable thinking of the day. Thus he recognised the vitality of Indian languages and the need to make them vehicles of education. Delivering the convocation address of the Telugu University in Hyderabad he referred to the "imperative need of rendering regional languages as effective media of communication and instruction."[9]

He went on to say: "It is a fact that right from the days of the national movement there was a constant demand for the enrichment of regional languages as instruments for administrative convenience and educational growth. Mahatma Gandhi made the development of regional languages a significant item in the national movement. Way back in 1928 he observed in a speech in Gujarat: "We may give a working knowledge of that (English) language, but we may not, without committing national suicide, neglect the mother tongue. We must enrich it and make it capable of expressions all shades of thought and feeling."[10]

Sharma shows that he is aware of the doubts entertained about the limitations of Indian languages in respect of higher learning but said: "There is a general apprehension that regional languages or mother tongues are not yet fully equipped to meet the challenges of modern times with the massive expansion of knowledge in all fields, particularly in science and technology. I would, however, endorse through my own experience connected with education, that by and large people are able to express themselves more effectively in their mother tongue, whatever may be their knowledge and scholarship in a foreign language".[11] He went on to quote Nehru who had observed in 1937 that "the masses can grow educationally and culturally through the medium of their own languages".[12] He called for the effective implementation of the three language formula proposed by the National Integration Council in 1962.

He has been a votary of the synthesis of our cultural attainments and of a catholic outlook. He spoke in praise of the position of Hyderabad city, of which he had first-hand knowledge as Governor of Andhra Pradesh State, in his Convocation address at the Telugu University in that city. He said: "Hyderabad is a miniature India, with its cosmopolitan nature, with people of many languages and religions. The city has a glorious history. In fact, with its geographical location, the State of Andhra Pradesh is described as the heartland of the country ....I am not interpreting the word(heartland) in the context of geography alone-but in a wider sense, in terms of the ethos of India, India's heritage of assimilation, synthesis and harmony, of tolerance and understanding and sturdy nationalism with a humanistic world view. The concept of आविभक्तं विभक्तेषु mentioned in the Gita - of the indivisible and the uniting element in the apparently divided - of unity in diversity, as Pandit Jawaharlal-Nehru expressed it, this concept is of the very essence of the history of our country and of Andhra Pradesh".[13]

This brings us to the major point in Sharma's thinking. A catholic outlook and keenness to perceive the uniting factors, combined with deep attachment to the values preached and practised by Nehru, are central to his scheme of things. Reverence for Nehru can be read in his speeches but it is not blind reverence of an unthinking mind. It has clearly grown out of his conviction that India was fortunate to have had the leadership of Nehru in the formative years after freedom and even in the struggle for freedom, as a devoted associate of Gandhi, Nehru's historical perspective, understanding of the forces that welded India together and his deep commitment to democratic values.

Sharma's choice of quotations from Nehru shows his abiding faith in the secular and democratic values dear to Nehru's heart. Speaking at a seminar in Trivandrum on "Nehru, Secularism and Minorities", Shanker Dayal recalled what Nehru had said in Parliament in August 1950 reacting to a suggestion on exchange of populations with the erstwhile East Pakistan, now Bangaldesh": ... This is a proposition which, if it is followed, will mean the ruin of India and the annihilation of all that we stand for and stood for. I repeat that we will resist such a proposition with all our strength, we will fight in houses, in fields and in market places. It will be fought in the council chambers and the streets, for we shall not let India be slughtered at the altar of bigotry."[14]

For Sharma, however, secularism does not exclude commitment to one's religion provided each one is free to pursue his faith and has respect for the other's faith. He, therefore, looks for and finds enough support for his belief that secularism and religious pursuit are not mutually exclusive. In this context his selection of a quotation from Nehru's Azad Memorial lecture of 1959 is particularly relevant. Nehru said in that, the first Azad Memorial lecture: "Four great religions have influenced India - two emerging from her own thought, Hinduism and Buddhism, and two coming from abroad but establishing themselves firmly in India, Christianity and Islam. Science today challenges the old concept of religion. But if religion deals not with dogmas and ceremonials, but rather with the higher things of life, there should be no conflict with science or *inter se* between religions. It must be the high privilege of India to help in bringing about their synthesis. That would be in India's ancient tradition inscribed on Ashoka's edicts."[15]

In a significant address on secularism delivered by Sharma, he delved deep into the Indian secular ethos in terms not only of the past but also its implications examined for the present and future. He spoke of the "immense ocean of secular experience and humanistic thought that is our common heritage."[16]

The occasion was the Zakir Hussain Memorial lecture delivered by Dr. Sharma, at Viswa Bharati, Shantiniketan, on April 29, 1989. He quoted, with approval, Mahatma Gandhi's observation on religion and secularism. Sharma said: "Communalism should not be confused with religion. The history of our secular ethos tells us so. The uplifting content of our great religions tells us so. That is why Mahatma Gandhi had said in "Young India" on November 27, 1924 - as far back as 1924 - "For me there is no politics without religion - not the religion of the superstitious and the blind religion that hates and fights, but the universal Religion of Toleration. Politics without morality is a thing to be avoided".[17]

Sharma goes on to explain: "Bapu thus fervently pleaded for political thought and action based on morality and ethics which all the religions have stood for. It is crucial, therefore, that we should understand that the real enemy of a healthy political environment is the outlook of communal mindedness - an outlook in which the morals and ethics of religion are absent."

Secularism to Dr. Sharma is *"Sarva Dharma Samabhava"*, equal regard for all religions. He said at the outset in his Zakir Hussain lecture:"We in India ... understand secularism to denote *"Sarva Dharma Samabhava"*: an approach of tolerance and understanding, of equality of all religions."[18]

He traces the seeds or secularism in the Indian ethos to the famous quotations from a Rigvedic verse: "
एक सद विप्रा बहुधा वदान्ति truth is one, the

learned speak (of it) variously". Says Dr. Sharma: "Thus a core idea of secular thought is expressed recognising the many paths of logical and intuitive access to Absolute Truth: acknowledging and providing conceptual basis to a philosophy of *Sarva Dharma Samabhava* whereby apparently different bodies of religious thought are seen as converging in the same, and only, truth."

Taking off from that point Shanker Dayal goes on to delineate the gradual manifestation of the thought in different works of religion like the Atharvaveda and Yajurveda and the Bhagwad Gita. He quotes copiously from these sources to underline the conclusion drawn by him that the secular outlook is basic to Indian religious thinking.

In the same address Sharma also pointed out that creative writers and thinkers like Rabindranath Tagore have strongly subscribed to this view. Referring to Tagore's Essay on the Vision of India he quoted the Gurudev to say : "I love India not because I cultivate the idolatry of geography, not because I have had the chance to be born in her soil, but because she has saved through tumultuous ages the living words that have issued from the illuminated consciousness of her great sons : Brahma is Truth. ... and the unity of all beings is in Brahma."[19]

The concept of '*Sarva Dharma Samabhava*' is beautifully expressed in an Ashokan edict (the Shahbazgarhi rock edict near Peshawar now in Pakistan) which says : "The increase of spiritual strength is of many forms. But the root is the guarding of one's speech so as to avoid the extolling of one's religion, or the decrying of the religion of another, or speaking lightly of it without occasion or relevance. As proper occasions arise, persons of other religions should also be honoured suitably .... One who revers one's own religion and disparages that of another from devotion to one's own religion and to glorify it over all other religions does injure one's own religion most certainly."[20]

Dr. Sharma did not forget to mention the Jain tradition as part of this systemic growth and explained how in such a climate of tolerance Christianity and Islam came to this land and were welcomed. "...the initial appearance of Christianity or Islam or Zorostrianism in India and their establishment on the mainland did not occur as a result of military conquest or threat of conquest. These religions were given a place by virtue of the attitude of accommoda-tion and co-existence displayed by local authorities—in-cluding the main religious authorities. The second aspect is even more important. Christianity, Islam and Zorostrianism brought with them spiritual and humanistic thought harmonious and, in fact, identical to the core ideas of the established religious thought in India as exemplified by the basic beliefs of Vedic, Vedantic, Buddhist and Jain philosophy."[21]

Contrary to the thinking of some sections which have seen a basic conflict between Islam and Hinduism, Sharma has repeatedly stressed the underlying coherence between the two. He observed in the same lecture: "The harmonious interaction between Hindu and Islamic culture reflected it-self not only in religious movements and philosophy but in language, literature, architecture, music and art—each emerging enriched."[22]

The rise of Sikhism and the growth of the Bhakti movement along with the role of Sufism have been ex-plained in some detail to underline Sharma's thesis that Indian tradition, although rooted in religion, has been basi-cally secular.

It was but natural that Gandhi would be copiously quoted in this context. Referring to the Mahatma's thinking

Shanker Dayal said: "Mahatma Gandhi's leadership and inner philosophical convictions were outstandingly powerful elements in promoting the secular outlook in India. Writing in the *Harijan* of May 14, 1938, he stated : 'Islam, it is said, believes in the brotherhood of man. But it is not the brotherhood of Muslims only, but universal brotherhood. The Allah of Islam is the same as the God of Christians and the Ishwara of the Hindus......." He wrote in *Hind Swaraj* : "The soul of religions is one, but it is encased in many forms."[23]

Sharma's study of this fascinating theme takes him to the thinking of yet another great son of India, Maulana Abul Kalam Azad who was a recognised authority on Islam. He quoted extensively from the Maulana's writings and said : ".... Maulana Abul Kalam Azad expositioned his interpretation of the true message of Islam. In his *Tarjuman*, Maulana Azad uses the very first words in the Quran Sharif, in the Al Fatiha, to explain the rationality of and spiritually appropriate position. Referring to the Al Fatiha, Maulana Azad asks : 'What will be the mental attitude of a person who sincerely believes in the letter and spirit of such a prayer?' And he explains : 'Such a person passionately chants the glory and praise of God—not a God claimed as their own by different races and nations and creeds, but the beneficent creator of the entire universe, whose mercy and compassion encompass the whole human race.'

"Then he prays for God's grace to follow the right path, the only favour his tongue is prepared to ask. And what is this right, this straight path? Is it the path of some particular nation or race? Or some particular group? No, it is the common path which all the great religious leaders of mankind, all the truth loving and truth seeking men and women of the world have trodden, whatever the age or race to which they belonged. Likewise he prays to be shielded from the path of transgression or wrong. But there, too, there is no reference to any particular race or creator or nation but to the ways of all those who have fallen from grace and been led astray. Thus what he passionately desires is the universal good of all mankind. What then is the kind of mould in which the mind of such a person will be cast ?He will worship the God of universal compassion and grace and will in no sense be a man fettered by prejudices of race or any other exclusive groupings. He will be a man endowed with spirit of universal humanism."[24]

NOTES

1. Published by Sterling Publishers, New Delhi, 1992.
2. Published by Prabhat Prakashan, Delhi, 1991.
3. Published by Nataraj Prakashan, Delhi, 1991
4. Sterling, 1989 and 1992.
5. *Horizons of Indian Education*, p.2.
6. *Ibid* p.2.
7. *Ibid* p.6.
8. *Ibid* p.6.
9. *Ibid* p.70.
10. *Ibid* pp.70-71.
11. *Ibid* p.71.
12. *Ibid* p.71.
13. *Ibid* p.69.
14. Jawaharlal Nehru p. 56.
15. *Ibid* pp. 56-57.
16. Printed booklet containing address obtained from Vice President's Office.
17. *Ibid*
18. *Ibid*

19. *Ibid*
20. *Ibid*
21. *Ibid*
22. *Ibid*
23. *Ibid*
24. *Ibid*

11

INDIA'S MR. CLEAN

Standards of morality in politics have taken a nosedive in the past several years. Scandals come tumbling out of the cupboards of politicians and only a few suffer for them, some of the others even managing to ride back to power after temporary oblivion. Amassing of wealth, misuse of position for personal gains and promoting one's kith and kin while in office are taken as the norms for politicians irrespective of their party affiliations, with some shining exceptions. Often, in the name of collecting funds for one's party huge sums are pocketed by politicians

Among the men and women who have emerged with a clean reputation after years in active politics is Shanker Dayal Sharma. His political career began way back in 1952 when Dr Sharma became the Chief Minister of Bhopal State, one of the part C States which existed on the political map of India until the States were reorganised in 1956, mostly on the basis of the State Reorganisation Commission(SRC)'s recommendations. When Bhopal as a consequence was merged with the larger Madhya Pradesh State in 1956, Dr Sharma was appointed a Cabinet minister and held important portfolios like education, industries and law.

He held Cabinet rank in the State for ten long years and then became President of the Madhya Pradesh Congress Committee in 1967, soon to be appointed a member of the Congress Working Committee and one of the general secretaries of the party. He later became President of the Congress and afterwards was a Cabinet Minister in the Union Government. From August 1984 he held a number of gubernatorial positions finally becoming India's Vice President in September 1987.

Much smaller men have been the focal point of corruption charges and have had their names linked with minor or major scandals. Dr Sharma has not only kept his copybook clean but also set high standards of probity and integrity in public life.

Bhopal was a comparatively small place when he took over as Chief Minister, succeeding Chatur Narayan Malaviya who had then shifted his activity to Parliament. Dr. Sharma was just 34 years of age but by virtue of his high academic attainments and his intellectual calibre he was destined to make a mark in his public life. The run-of-the-mill politician would have found ample opportunities to make monetary gains for himself in such a career.

Not Shanker Dayal, who chose to tread the narrow and difficult path of honesty in politics while proving himself a highly efficient and successful minister and politician. Land grab has been the easiest way for a politician to make money as urban land prices have been continuously escalating. Other politicians have made money—some have virtually minted it—by award of contracts and licences and in the selection of tenderers for major construction or similar jobs.

Shanker Dayal kept from the path of temptation all through. Since he had hardly had time to settle down in any profession before he took up full time politics as a career and because he had not inherited any large ancestral property, Sharma had very limited private means. There were quite a few periods in life when he held no public office and the family found it difficult to make two ends meet.

A senior journalist, K.P. Srivastava[1], who has known Dr. Sharma from the days of his Bhopal tenure as Chief Minister, when he came to be posted as PTI correspondent in Bhopal in 1954, says, "Sharma lived in a two rooms house in Bhopal when out of office. Even in Delhi when he held no official or party position, he lived in two small rooms in the guest house of a business concern of his '*sambandhi*' (a person related to one by the marriage of one's son or daughter). In one room, his belongings were dumped as though it was some kind of a *Kabarikhana* (a junk shop) and in the other Sharma lived himself with some members of his family."

There could be no better example of the spartan way of life he had preferred than the manner in which the higher education of his second son, Ashutosh, was terminated after he had done his B.A. Srivastava who knew the family at close quarters pleaded with Dr. Sharma to allow 'Bablu' (as Ashutosh was known) to keep terms for his M.A. Says Srivastava: "Sharma told me he had calculated the college fees, hostel fees and other expenses and said they were beyond him."[2]

Another instance which Srivastava recalled was what happened when Shanker Dayal was Congress President (1972-74) and a large team of young men and women was being deputed to Moscow for one of the youth festivals which the Soviets used to sponsor for the third world countries before their country folded up. Sharma's daughter, Geetanjali, was an active student leader in Delhi University and was holding a key position in the students' union. In other words she was quite qualified to be in the Indian squad. But Sharma would not put in a word for her with the authorities concerned with the selection of "delegates" to the Moscow festival. At Geetanjali's instance Srivastava himself spoke to the authorities but Sharma refused to raise his little finger on his daughter's behalf.[3]

Geetanjali fell to the assassin's bullet in 1985, along with her husband, Lalit Maken, then a Delhi MP unidentified Punjab terrorists gunned down the couple when both were meeting Lalit Maken's constituents in West Delhi. The motive was suspected to be the alleged involvement of Maken in the terrible anti-Sikh riots in Delhi in November 1984 in the wake of Mrs Gandhi's murder by two of her Sikh bodyguards.

That was a severe blow to Dr. Sharma, something which could have made lesser mortals go under. Sharma, however, survived the tragedy. He was then Andhra Pradesh Governor. He took the tragic loss of his dearly loved daughter in such circumstances with stoicism and resignation, seeking solace in the Gita which teaches one how to carry out one's duties and go on doing one's allotted task whatever the circumstances.

One of his younger brothers, Ish Dayal, told the *Sunday Mail*[4] of Delhi in interview in July 1992 that *"Dadabhai"* as the eldest brother, Shanker Dayal, is fondly called by the family, had over-ruled Ish's nomination for fighting the

1990 Madhya Pradesh Assembly poll on the Congress(I) ticket. Ish Dayal told the paper's correspondent that both Arjun Singh and Moti Lal Vora, former Chief Ministers and leading lights of the State Congress(I), had okayed his nomination but when the two of them consulted Shanker Dayal he put his feet down.

"...the final nod had to come from Doctor Sahib. When they (Singh and Vora) spoke to *Dadabhai* he negatived it outright. When I came to know of it I felt bad. But he called me up the next day and explained to me why he had done so. He told me that I was still a novice in politics and had a lot to learn," Ish Dayal is reported to have told the paper.

According to the interview, Shanker Dayal had also a practical reason why his younger brother should stay away from the assembly poll. "He told me it was not the right time to fight because the political climate was not favourable to the Congress. In fact, he told me that the party would win only 40- odd seats."[5] The Congress actually won 56 seats in a house of 319 members and the BJP won the election with a handsome majority of 219 seats. Sharma's assessment of his former party's prospects was not much off the mark (former party, because once he was elected Vice- President he had ceased to be partyman.)

In his Hindi book "Mukhya Mantri Madhya Pradesh Ke", Mayaram Surjan, who as a newspaper man and publisher enjoyed close relations with the politicians of the State, has dealt with Shanker Dayal's tenure as Chief Minister of Bhopal and as a Cabinet Minister in Madhya Pradesh State.

Surjan recalls how Sharma lived in a two small rooms house in Professor's colony in Bhopal, once the Congress lost power in the State and he ceased to be a minister in 1967. Says Surjan: "Despite Dr. Sharma's indifference to the party workers, no blame can be attached to him directly.

Come to think of it, hundreds of allegations can be levelled against every politician or office holder. But I cannot recall a single instance when any blame had been laid at Dr. Sharma's door. In 1967 when the (D.P.) Mishra ministry fell (for Madhya Pradesh) Dr. Sharma went and lived in his small house in Professor's colony. No show of any dignity, no complaint. When he entered the Lok Sabha he again lived in this house."[6]

Surjan also narrates an incident when he met Dr. Sharma after he had left the Bhopal scene. Sharma greeted Surjan and forgot how as a publisher he had opposed Sharma while he was in office, "Doctor Sahib had almost forgotten my opposition to him. Some years ago I met him in his office in the AICC(I). He was then Chairman of the Twenty Point Programme Committee. He adjusted the appointments of other visitors and kept on talking to me for three hours.... When I met him in the Bhopal Rajnivas (Governor's residence) last September (1985), I conveyed my sympathies to him over the killing of his daughter Geetanjali and son-in-law Lalit Maken. He wept like a child. He was then Governor of Andhra Pradesh. Those moments of intimacy can hardly be forgotten. Once when I reminded him of my adversary position in his career in Bhopal he said, "Forget about it. ....." This single sentence wiped out the entire bad blood."[7]

It is not as though no blemish has ever attached to him. In a long career spread over so many years, some actions and statements could certainly be found when Dr. Sharma could not have measured up to his own exacting standards. But even his critics have not been able to find any notable instance where he was found wanting.

The Emergency proclaimed by Mrs. Gandhi in June 1975 (lifted only in January 1977 when general elections were announced) has been cited by some in which

Dr. Sharma had not shown a capacity for standing up for the high democratic values to which he is deeply committed.

Undoubtedly, the Emergency is a blot on the career of Mrs. Gandhi and those who were associated with her and played an active role during the nineteen months when the country was ruled virtually by decree and under strict censorship. But the fact has to be noted that people sometimes have double standards in judging the main characters of that period.

Take Jagjivan Ram for example. He was Minister of Agriculture and Irrigation and occupied a virtual No.2 place in the hierarchy, although Indira was shrewd enough neither to groom nor let anyone get away with the feeling that he was being groomed for succession. Jagjivan Ram was not only a party to the Emergency and its proclamation but even moved the resolution in the Lok Sabha for approval of the Emergency proclamation on July 21, 1975, within less than a month of the Emergency being enforced. He spoke enthusiastically in support of the motion moved by him, not with any apology or regrets for what had happened.

The motion was adopted on July 22[8] and after its adoption by the upper house it gave the seal of Parliamentary approval to the unworthy deed. Yet, when Jagjivan Ram resigned from Mrs. Gandhi's cabinet and her party on February 2, 1977, just a month and a half before the general elections were to take place and when Mrs. Gandhi looked like losing her mandate in the trial of strength that was due shortly, his action was hailed in the media and he was enthusiastically welcomed by the Janata Party leaders. He later on became a senior minister in the Morarji cabinet and even rose to be a Deputy Prime Minister. Jagjivan Ram had jumped on to the Jayaprakash bandwagon when the going was good.

Jagjivan Ram is not known to have been accused of opportunism, nor his role in the Emergency recalled. There are others who played an approving role in the Emergency although they were not assigned nor did they seek an active part in its proclamation or in running the country during that period. Among them was no less a person than Vishwanath Pratap Singh who was a junior minister in the Indira Gandhi Council of Ministers in 1975-77.

This is not said in justification of Dr. Sharma's meek acquiesence in the Emergency rule and continuing as part of the Government during that time. All that can be said is that Dr. Sharma had the good fortune not to be associated with any kind of excesses of the Emergency, like putting down the political opponents with a heavy hand, forcing family planning down the people's threats and suppressing the media.

Ironically the politician who had a big hand in media (mis)management during the Emergency, Vidya Charan Shukla, from Shanker Dayal's native Madhya Pradesh, is now a cabinet minister in the Narasimha Rao Government. In between he had left Rajiv Gandhi and had even accused him of involvement in the Bofors deal, joined the Janata Dal, defected from the main JD to Chandra Shekhar's breakaway group and become the Minister of External Affairs in that shortlived government, only to be disqualified by the Speaker of the Lok Sabha.

There is some moral in the fact that Dr. Sharma's eighty- year-old mother, Sampatbai, still lives in the ancestral house in old Bhopal's Guliya Dai Ka Mohalla where he was born and brought up. Most other politicians would have not only shifted the family residence to some exclusive neighbourhood of Bhopal, or even Delhi, and Sampatbai would have become an adviser in Indian medicine to the Central Government or the Government of Madhya Pradesh.

The house is also not much different from what it was. It is a double storey house and in a small room on the ground floor the Ayurvedic clinic inherited by Sampatbai from Dr. Sharma's father, Pandit Khushilal, is being run for the better part of the day. Under the prevailing norms for any top figure in the ruling party, the house would be totally renovated and the neighbours would have run for shelter elsewhere as their land would have been acquired for the family, in the name perhaps of providing medical facilities to the "weaker sections" of society living in old Bhopal.

NOTES

1. K.P.Srivastava worked in different capacities for the Press Trust of India(PTI) and retired some years ago as Chief News Editor, PTI Headquarters, New Delhi. He was also Information Adviser to Prime Minister Chandra Shekhar.

   In Personal communication to the author.
2. *Ibid*
3. *Ibid*
4. *Sunday Mail*, Delhi, July 12, 1992. Interview by Swapna Majumdar.
5. *Ibid*
6. "Mukhya Mantri Madhya Pradesh Ke", Mayaram Surjan, published by Radhakrishna Prakashan, Delhi, 1991

   See chapter on Dr. Sharma, pp 60–75.
7. *Ibid*
8. *Parliament of India-The Fifth Lok Sabha-A study*, S.L. Shakdhar, published by Lok Sabha Secretariat, Delhi, 1977

12

MANY-FACETED PERSONALITY

Dr. Shanker Dayal Sharma achieved high distinctions in his studies which could well be the envy of any scholar. He was, however, no bookworm. A sound physique and the early training he received at the hands of his father in his days in Bhopal inculcated in him a love of sports and games. He won several nonours as a sportsman in the university and excelled in athletics, rowing and swimming. He was the swimming champion in Lucknow University for three years running. He was also captain of the Rowing and Swimming Club of the University and later became its president.

At his age of 74 years, it is no longer possible for him to keep up with athletics, or swimming. He is, however, fond of long walks in his spacious garden. Among the games he played in his younger days was also badminton.

International law, international affairs, constitutional law and problems relating to that, legislative procedures and practices and detailed study of political parties and their organisational structure have always been of special interest to Dr. Sharma. He has also written extensively on these subjects, apart from religion, philosophy and the art and culture of India.

His publications include:

Congress Approach to International Affairs, Kranti Drashta, Indo-Soviet Relations, Rule of Law and Role of Police, Readings in Indo-Soviet Friendship and Co-operation, Jawaharlal Nehru-Selected speeches, Eminent Indians, Hamare Path Pradarshak, Horizons of Indian Education and Deshmani.

He has also contributed a number of articles on different subjects to national and international journals. He held a number of editorial assignments and among the journals he edited were :

Lucknow Law Journal (1941–43), *Light and Learning* (1942-43), *Ilm-o-Noor (Urdu), Jyoti (Hindi), and Socialist India* (1971-74).

Dr. Sharma has had abiding interest in education, despite his full time political career. He was a teacher in the Law School in Lucknow University. His official position as Minister in Madhya Pradesh and as Governor of several States and Vice-President of India brought him important assignments in the educational field. From 1956 to 1959, he was Pro-Chancellor of Sagar University in Madhya Pradesh. As Governor of Andhra Pradesh, he also discharged responsibilities of Chancellor of Andhra University, Sri Venkateswara University, Nagarjuna University, Kakatiya University, Jawaharlal Nehru Technological University, Osmania University, Sri Krishna Devaraya

University, Padmavati Women's University and also acted as Rector of the University of Hyderabad.

Likewise his tenure as Governor of Punjab and Maharashtra brought him in close contact with the universities in these two advanced States. In Punjab, he was the Chancellor of Punjabi University, Guru Nanak Dev University and Punjab Agricultural University. While he was Governor of Maharashtra, he was Chancellor of the Universities of Bombay and Poona, SNDT Women's University, Nagpur University, Marathwada University, Shivaji University, Amravati University, Punjabrao Krishi Vidyapeeth, Konkan Krishi Vidyapeeth, Mahatma Phule Krishi Vidyapeeth, and Marathwad Krishi Vidyapeeth.

While he was holding the office of Vice President of India he had also to perform the duties of the Chancellor of Delhi University, Punjab University, Pondicherry University, Gandhigram Rural Institute (a Deemed University) and as visitor of Makhanlal Chaturvedi Rashtriya Vishwavidyalaya Sansthan, Bhopal.

The important thing to note is that Dr. Shanker Dayal Sharma's personality made for harmonious and amicable relations between the Chancellor and the Universities concerned. Too often we are familiar with ex-officio, chancellors and the educational institutions working at loggerheads.

From time to time Dr. Sharma was called upon to deliver the convocation address of a number of Universities in India. The list includes :

Madras University, Sri Sathya Sai Institute of Higher Learning, Puttupurthy (A deemed University), Agra University, Kendriya Sanskrit Vidyapeeth, Tirupati, Bombay University, Tata Institute of Social Science, Bombay (a Deemed University), Gandhigram Rural Institute (a

Deemed University), Sardar Patel University, Indian Institute of Management, Calcutta, Indian Institute of Foreign Trade, New Delhi, Telugu University, Hyderbad, Devi Ahilya Vishwavidyalaya, Indore, Goa University, Goa, University of Roorkee, and Indira Gandhi National Open University.

His High academic distinctions and exalted position in public life also brought him a number of honorary degrees from several universities including one from the University of Mauritius, Doctor of Civil Law (Honoris Causa). The honorary Degree of Law was conferred on him by the Vikram University, Bhopal University, Agra University, Sri Venkateswara University, Tirupati and Devi Ahilya Vishwavidyalaya, Indore. The University of Roorkee honoured him with the Degree of Doctor of Social Sciences while Meerut University awarded the Honorary Degree of Doctor of Literature.

It has become a practice among the politicians in India to flaunt their honorary degrees and many of them adorn their names with the prefix "Dr.".This is against the well recognised convention that an honorary degree does not entitle the receiver to call himself "Dr.". In Dr. Sharma's case, however, the problem never arose, because he had from his early life earned a Ph.D. from Cambridge University.

As Vice President, Dr. Sharma was called upon to head the Indian Council for Cultural Relations, New Delhi, as its president. He was also President of the Indian Institute of Public Administration in New Delhi. Dr. Sharma also headed the jury which select outstanding personalities from the world for the Jawaharlal Nehru Award for International Understanding. He was also chairman of the International Jury for the Indira Gandhi Prize for Peace, Disarmament and Development. When the Rajiv Gandhi

Foundation was set up in 1991, he was appointed one of the trustees.

Dr. Sharma is noted for his even temperament and the smile he wears on his face is a genuine expression of his courtesy and friendly approach. He has always been a low profile whether he was holding ministerial responsibilities or Constitutional positions like Governor and Vice President of India. That, however, did not prevent him for taking firm decisions, for example, when he faced dissidents early in his career in Bhopal or as Governor of Andhra Pradesh when he had no hesitation in dismissing the pretender Chief Minister Bhaskara Rao and reinstalled N.T. Ram Rao, the only case of its kind where a dismissed Chief Minister was reinstated.

Also as Vice President when he presided over the Rajya Sabha he displayed firmness when faced with rowdyism by some members and defiance by Ministers and members of the ruling party.

A deeply religious person, who holds that Indian seculiarism has to be based on each one pursuing his religious faith and respecting the faiths of others. Dr. Sharma spends some time every day in his *'Puja'* room. He is also a frequent visitor to the famous shrine of Sri Venkateswara at Tirupati in Andhra Pradesh. In fact he has visited a number of religious places in south India as well as other parts of the country and met the men of religion. In Tamil Nadu he has visited the abode of the Shankaracharya at Kanchi Kamakoti as well as the Ahobila Mutt. He has made a special study of ancient Tamil works and often quotes the words of wisdom and religious significance from them : "I see the Almighty everywhere", Dr. Shanker Dayal has said so often.

Even the most composed and collected person sometimes may lapse momentarily into a display of annoyance or even anger. One such occasion was when Dr. Sharma was on his way to Tirupati from Madras. Accompanying him were a few journalists and his grandchildren, among them Avantika, the only child of his slain daughter Geetanjali and son-in-law Lalit Makan, who were both gunned down by the terrorists. While the VIP aircraft was touching down at Tirupati, one of the grandchildren (not Avantika) reported the loss of a wristwatch. Dr. Sharma left the plane to fulfil his engagements at the Tirupati Veda Sadas, giving instructions to the pilot to look for the watch.

On his return to the plane he was informed that the watch had not been found, although the crew and the ground staff had searched high and low for it. This was one moment when Dr. Sharma was visibly angered and he gave a piece of his mind to the crew. His annoyance was both due to the fact that the grand-child would be missing her favourite watch and also due to the negligence of the crew in a VIP aircraft where even a pin should be located if it was mislaid.[1]

On occasions, as we have seen, Dr. Sharma displayed emotion. He shed tears when he read out his message of thanks on his election as President and referred to Mahatma Gandhi and other leaders whose ideals he would try to uphold as President. That even people in such high positions are subject to human emotions needs hardly to be stressed.

NOTE

1. R. Rajagopalan, Correspondent of *Dinamani*, Madras, in personal communication to the author.

Being sworn in as Ninth President of India by Chief Justice M.H. Kania on July 25, 1992.

With Pakistan Prime Minister Nawaz Sharif on the latter's visit to Delhi to attend Rajiv Gandhi's funeral.

With Dr S. Radhakrishnan in Indore, M.P.

With Chinese Prime Minister Le Peng, during the latter's visit to Delhi.

Taking Lal Bahadur Shastri's ashes for immersion in the Narmada at Hoshangabad(M.P.) as a Senior Minister in the State.

With Julius Nyerere.

With Guyana Prime Minister Huga Desmond Hoyte in Georgetown.

Greeting Prime Minister P. V. Narasimha Rao on his birthday in 1991.

With Nelson Mandela

Dr. Sharma as Minister of Communications.

Appendix I

INAUGURAL ADDRESS

On July 25, 1992 Dr Shanker Dayal Sharma was sworn in the ninth President of India in the Central Hall of Parliament House by the Chief Justice of India, Mr Justice M.H. Kania. The outgoing President, Mr R. Venkataraman, the Speaker of the Lok Sabha, Mr Shivraj Patil, the Deputy Chairman of the Rajya Sabha, Mrs Najma Heptulla, the Prime Minister, Mr P.V. Narasimha Rao, his cabinet colleagues, members of Parliament, Mrs. Vimla Sharma, Dr Sharma's mother, Mrs Sampatbai, and several other distinguished persons were present to witness the historic ceremony.

In an emotion-choked voice Dr Sharma read his address to the assembled gathering after the swearing in. It was carried live by AIR and Doordarshan. The address is as follows :

On having entered upon the office of the President of our Republic, I stand before you, in all humility, overwhelmed with gratitude for the honour done to me in electing me to a position graced by such illustrious personages as Dr. Rajendra Prasad, Dr. Sarvepalli Radhakrishnan and Dr. Zakir Husain. The stalwarts who have preceded me devoted their great personal qualities to national well-being, striving with utmost dedication to perform the role assigned in our polity to the Constitutional Head of State.

My mind is filled with thoughts of the Father of our Nation, Mahatma Gandhi, and the great national leaders, martyrs and freedom fighters, whose suffering and sacrifices made freedom possible and helped build our country's system of Parliamentary Democracy.

May I say that I shall endeavour to do all I may, in keeping with the oath I have had the honour to make and subscribe, to serve our Nation in a manner as would befit an occupant of this office.

I have given expression to these thoughts after some deliberation, aware that there is cause for introspection also by all who wish to take this great country forward—all who yearn to see an India as a land of peace, harmony, prosperity and social justice : a strong, united nation, wedded to the Rule of Law, drawing sustenance from ethical and moral values, and capable thus of over-coming the challenges of terrorism, communal feeling, and caste and gender oppression, of poverty, ignorance and disease.

We are in the fiftieth year after the Quit India Movement of 1942 and memories flood my mind of the idealism, courage and determination with which the great struggle was waged. We have to safeguard freedom and the gains of freedom. Let us remember that freedom has little meaning without equality, and equality has little meaning without social and economic justice. During my term in office I hope and pray that I would witness the needs and concerns of the people being ministered to, and a much better quality of life materialising, particularly in the rural areas where, for many, each day is filled with worry about livelihood, sustenance and security.

And as we strive for national reconstruction, the vision of great leaders in our history is with us : of India's role in the comity of nations. On August 14, 1947, speaking in the Constituent Assembly, in the emerging moments of Independent India. Pandit Jawaharlal Nehru had said : "We have to labour and to work to give reality to our dreams. Those dreams are also for the world, for all the nations and the peoples. Peace has been said to be indivisible; so is freedom, so is prosperity now, and so also is disaster in this One World that can no longer be split into isolated fragments."

Fellow citizens, our ethos of secularism—equal respect for all religions—involving a concept and a way of life which every Indian should naturally understand, ought to guide us every day in our individual growth and social inter-action as a time-tested approach for the attainment of our cherished goals.

Gurudev Rabindranath Tagore, in an Essay on the Vision of India, had been moved to say :"I love India, not because I cultivate the idolatry of geography, not because I have had the chance to be born in her soil, but because she has saved through tumultuous ages the living words that have issued from the illuminated consciousness of her great sons."

Over fifty centuries ago, in the Prithvi Sukta in the Atharva Veda, we find a magnificent manifestation on our secular outlook :

"जनं बिभ्रती बहुधा विवाचसम् । नानाधर्माणं पृथिवो यथौकसम् ।"

(The Earth which supports diverse people of various persuasions and temperaments, as in a peaceful home, may it benefit all of us.)

The Yajurveda states · मित्रस्य चक्षुषा समीक्षामहे । ।

(May we look on one another with the eyes of a friend.)

The Bhagwad Gita states :

"ये यथा मां प्रपद्यन्ते तांस्तथैव भजाम्यहम् ।
मम वर्त्मानुवर्तन्ते मनुष्याः पार्थ सर्वशः । ।"

(In whatever way men identity with Me, in the same way do I carry out their desires; *men pursue My path, Partha, in all ways.*)

An exquisite expression of secular dictates, stemming from Buddhist thought may be secured from Edict-XII of the Mauryan Emperor Ashoka :

> "One who reveres one's own religion and disparages that of another from devotion to one's own religion and to glorify it over all other religions, does injure one's own religion most certainly."

The Jain spiritual and intellectual tradition of universal love towards all living things, compassion and service, augments such a view. The immortal work, Thirukkural, by the Saint Thiruvalluvar, similarly commends an outlook of pluralism and oneness.

India received the light of Christianity as early as 52 A.D. when St. Thomas the Apostle preached the gospel in Kerala. This was centuries before Christianity reached Europe.

Some years ago I had occasion personally to tend upon Khan Abdul Ghaffar Khan—Badshah Khan, the heroic champion of freedom, non-violence and peace, who had a profound understanding of Islam. He used to say :

"मैंने सेक्युलरिज्म गांधी से नहीं सीखा। सेक्युलरिज्म मैंने कुरान में पाया।"

(I did not have to learn secularism from Gandhiji. I gained knowledge of secularism from the Qur'aan Sharief.)

His view in this respect coincided beautifully with the brilliant interpretation by Maulana Abul Kalam Azad in his Tarjuman Al Qur'aan and in his other writings.

The philosophy of Sikhism provides a superlative example of secular thought. Should all in India not bear in mind a verse composed by Guru Gobind Singh:

देहुरा मसीत सोई, पूजा ओ नमाज ओई,
मानस सभै ऐक पै अनेक को प्रभाव है।
अलह अभेख सोई, पुरान ओ कुरान ओई,
ए ऐक ही सरूप सभै, एक ही बनाव है।

(Mandir or Mosque, Puja or Namaz, Puran or Qur'aan have no difference. All human beings are equal and manifestations of the same.)

The appreciation by citizens of the oneness of the inner doctrine of all religions is essential as much for national well-being, as for the value of the contribution India can make to global understanding, peace and progress. Dr. Zakir Husain had once said :

> "We want peace between the individual and groups within nations. These are all vitally interdependent. If the spirit of the Sermon on the Mount, Buddha's philosophy of compassion, the Hindu concept of Ahimsa, and the passion of Islam for obedience to the will of God can combine, then we would succeed in generating the most potent influence for world peace."

At this moment I am aware, more than ever, that all of us, fellow citizens, have a great cause to serve. Great causes make great demands on the human spirit. If we are truly Indian in thought, action and spirit, we shall certainly illumine for the world the path to synthesis, harmony, peace and prosperity, and thus, indeed, be able to interpret the human spirit to all humankind.

I pray that the Almighty gives me the strength and wisdom to dedicate myself in the spirit of service for the proper fulfilment of my duties and responsibilities; and that our Nation advances from strength to strength, true to the genius and heritage of our people, for a better world, a better future, for all.

JAI HIND

Appendix II

BROADCAST TO THE NATION

In his broadcast to the nation on July 24, 1992, the outgoing President Mr. R. Venkataraman, paid a handsome tribute to his successor. He said:

"It is a matter of deep personal satisfaction to me that Dr. Shanker Dayal Sharma has been elected the next President of India. An eminent scholar well versed in Sanskrit, an erudite jurist not only by learning but also by his vast experience, a tried and tested veteran in the cause of national integrity and unity, and above all, a dedicated worker devoted to the welfare of the weaker sections of society, Dr. Sharma brings to bear on the high office of the President all the qualities that would go to make his tenure an unqualified success. I wish him a smooth and pleasant term as the Head of State. I appeal to you friends to extend to him not only your cooperation, but your kindness and affection."

Appendix III

MILESTONES IN DR SHARMA'S LIFE

August 19, 1918	Born in Bhopal
1935 to 1943	Studied at St. John's College, Agra, Allahabad University and Lucknow University and Secured M.A. and LL.M. Degrees
1943 to 1952	Lecturer/Reader, Department of Law, Lucknow University. In between went to Cambridge and Harvard. Did Ph.D. at Cambridge.
October 16, 1948	Returned to Bhopal from abroad after completing his studies

1948-49	Participated in agitation in Bhopal for princely State's merger with rest of India. Was imprisoned.
June 1, 1949	Bhopal merges with India
May 7, 1950	Married Vimla Sharma
January 11, 1951	Elected unopposed to presidentship of Bhopal Congress Committee
March, 1952	Elected to Bhopal assembly from Bairasiya constituency
March 20, 1952	Became first Chief Minister of Bhopal, Part 'C' State
November 1, 1956 to March 1967	Minister of Education, Public Works, Commerce and Industry in Madhya Pradesh Cabinet. Was elected to State Assembly from Udaypura constituency in 1957 and 1962.
1967	Elected President, Madhya Pradesh Congress Commitee
1968	Appointed member of the Congress Working Committee by President S. Nijalingappa and made one of the General Secretaries by him.
1969	After Congress split in later part of 1969 became general secretary of Congress(R), led by Mrs Gandhi
1971	Elected to Lok Sabha from Bhopal constituency
1972-74	President of the Indian National Congress, led by Mrs Gandhi

1974-77	Minister of Communications in Mrs Gandhi's Cabinet
March 1977	Lost election to Lok Sabha
December 1979	Elected to Lok Sabha from Bhopal
August 1984	Appointed Governor of Andhra Pradesh
November 1985	Governor of Punjab
April 3, 1986	Governor of Maharashtra
September 3, 1987	Sworn in as Vice President of India after unanimous election
July 25, 1992	Sworn in as President of India after winning election by a big margin

INDEX